"Would the Insects Inherit the Earth?"

Pergamon Titles of Related Interest

Davis ASYMMETRIES IN U.S. & SOVIET STRATEGIC DEFENSE PROGRAMS
Kelleher et al. NUCLEAR DETERRENCE
Leventhal & Alexander NUCLEAR TERRORISM
McNaught NUCLEAR WEAPONS & THEIR EFFECTS
Mayers UNDERSTANDING NUCLEAR WEAPONS & ARMS CONTROL
Windass AVOIDING NUCLEAR WAR

Related Journal

(Free specimen copy available upon request)

Defense Analysis

DISCLAIMER

Statements and opinions expressed in publications of the Health Physics Society or in presentations given during its regular meetings are those of the author(s) and do not necessarily reflect the official position of the Health Physics Society, the editors, or the organizations with which the authors are affiliated. The editors, publisher, and Society disclaim any responsibility or liability for such material and do not guarantee, warrant or endorse any product or service mentioned. Official positions of the Health Physics Society are established only by its Board of Directors.

"Would the Insects Inherit the Earth?"

And Other Subjects of Concern to Those Who Worry About Nuclear War

Compiled and Edited by
Jack C. Greene & **Daniel J. Strom**
Health Physics Society

PERGAMON PROFESSIONAL PUBLISHERS
An Imprint of Pergamon-Brassey's
International Defense Publishers, Inc.
(a member of the Pergamon Group)

Washington New York London Oxford Moscow
Beijing Frankfurt São Paulo Sydney Tokyo Toronto

U.S.A. (Editorial)	Pergamon-Brassey's International Defense Publishers, 8000 Westpark Drive, Fourth Floor, McLean, Virginia 22102, U.S.A.
(Orders)	Pergamon-Brassey's, Maxwell House, Fairview Park, Elmsford, New York 10523, U.S.A.
U.K. (Editorial)	Brassey's Defence Publishers, 24 Gray's Inn Road, London WC1X 8HR
(Orders)	Brassey's Defence Publishers, Headington Hill Hall, Oxford OX3 0BW, England
PEOPLE'S REPUBLIC OF CHINA	Pergamon Press, Room 4037, Qianmen Hotel, Beijing, People's Republic of China
FEDERAL REPUBLIC OF GERMANY	Pergamon Press, Hammerweg 6, D-6242 Kronberg, Federal Republic of Germany
BRAZIL	Pergamon Editora, Rua Eça de Queiros, 346, CEP 04011, Paraiso, São Paulo, Brazil
AUSTRALIA	Pergamon-Brassey's Defence Publishers, P.O. Box 544, Potts Point, N.S.W. 2011, Australia
JAPAN	Pergamon Press, 8th Floor, Matsuoka Central Building, 1-7-1 Nishishinjuku, Shinjuku-ku, Tokyo 160, Japan
CANADA	Pergamon Press Canada, Suite No. 271, 253 College Street, Toronto, Ontario, Canada M5T 1R5

Copyright © 1988 Health Physics Society

All Rights Reserved. No part of this publication may be reproduced, stored in a retrieval system or transmitted in any form or by any means, electronic, electrostatic, magnetic tape, mechanical, photocopying, recording or otherwise, without permission in writing from the publishers.

First printing 1988
Printed in the USA

Library of Congress Cataloging in Publication Data

```
Would the insects inherit the earth?

    Bibliography: p.
    Includes index.
    1. Nuclear warfare--Environmental aspects.  2. Nuclear
warfare--Physiological effect.  3. Nuclear warfare--
Psychological aspects.  4. Nuclear warfare--Safety
measures.  5. Radioactive fallout.  6. Civil defense.
7. Nuclear winter.  I. Greene, Jack C.   II. Strom,
Daniel J.
U263.W685  1987     574.5'222     87-29121
ISBN 0-08-035970-1 (soft)
```

Based on backup material developed for the Health Physics Society Summer School, "Health Physics Aspects of Nuclear Attack," held at Southeastern Louisiana University, Hammond, LA, May 28 - June 1, 1984.

PREFACE

This is a book about nuclear weapons, nuclear war and Civil Defense. But it is not an "all-about" book. Rather, it identifies key questions and provides discussions about them by knowledgeable people--many of whom are nationally and internationally known. The questions were selected from those that over the years most frequently have arisen when nuclear war and Civil Defense subjects were being discussed and to which, typically, incomplete or wrong answers were given. The value of the book, then, lies not so much in its breadth or scope, but in its focus and in the quality and variety of the material covered. We hope that this book will be useful to many readers--not only to those who have a personal concern about the subject matter but also those at various levels of government or in private enterprise who bear responsibilities for the safety and security of others.

Suggestions about using the book

As a starter, we suggest that the reader turn to the CONTENTS pages and become familiar with the identities of the respondents and the kinds of subjects they address. A brief biographical sketch about each appears starting on page 61. The reader may be especially interested in what a particular respondent has to say about the subject(s) he addresses.

Then, we suggest that the reader review the SUBJECT INDEX to find out what topics are covered and where they are to be found. Also, we suggest use of the document as a reference and as a source of quotable "statements by the experts" about specialized, and frequently controversial, nuclear-war-related subjects. It can help provide perspective.

Readers who would like to improve their general knowledge about nuclear weapons and the nuclear war threat are urged to consult reference documents such as those listed starting on page 73.

Background

"WOULD THE INSECTS INHERIT THE EARTH?" AND OTHER SUBJECTS OF CONCERN TO THOSE WHO WORRY ABOUT NUCLEAR WAR is a spinoff from one of the regularly scheduled activities of the Health Physics Society (HPS). This Society, an organization of approximately 6000 members, is devoted to the development of scientific knowledge and practical means for protection of man and his environment from harmful effects of radiation. A formal means for disseminating scientific findings is provided by the Society through its publications, in particular *Health Physics*, the official journal of the Health Physics Society, and its *Newsletter*. In addition to an annual meeting and other special meetings on timely subjects, each year the Society sponsors a summer school on some subject of special concern to its members. In 1984, the subject for the summer school was "Health Physics Aspects of Nuclear Attack."

The committee planning the school curriculum recognized a need to bring together widely scattered information pertaining to the school topic and to make it available to the school faculty and students. We, Jack Greene and Dan Strom, agreed to help. To augment our own ideas, we solicited, by means of a letter to the editor of the *HPS Newsletter*, suggestions about additional subject matter and potential respondents.

This letter brought many favorable responses and suggestions. Several people identified questions for which they volunteered to provide answers.

By the time of the summer school, some 23 respondents had prepared and submitted answers to some 34 questions. These manuscripts, in rough form, were handed out to faculty and students over the course of the school. During and after the course, additional topics were identified. In most cases we were able to find an expert to provide comments but in some cases we were not; nor could we hope to identify all of the subject matter that might be of interest to every reader. The field is too vast and too complex. We gave up any idea of being all-inclusive. This document contains just what its title suggests: "subjects of concern to those who worry about nuclear war."

Jack C. Greene
Daniel J. Strom

ACKNOWLEDGEMENTS

We could not be more complimentary about the efforts of the people who contributed answers to the questions. Because much of the research in this general area has been phased out due to lack of funding, most of the investigators have gone on to work in other fields. Therefore, in preparing their answers it became necessary for many of the respondents to consult old notebooks and technical reports and otherwise refresh their memories. There was a lot of work involved. Furthermore, many were asked to speculate a bit. This was in recognition of the fact that in some cases little hard data exist. (We all hope there will never be the kind of hard data that could only come from the actual experience of an nuclear attack.)

Also, we are pleased to acknowledge the contributions of Laurie Taylor, for his succinct commentary in the Foreword; John Tolan, for numerous suggestions, editing, and for publicity in the HPS *Newsletter*; Denise Miller, who did much of the word processing; Homer C. Tolan, Ph.D., for her aid in preparing the manuscript by redacting and copy editing, as well as designing the format; Roger Cloutier, Paul Stansbury, and Clayton French, fellow HPS members for their support, suggestions, and cooperation; and last, but by no means least, Michel Pawlowski, Carl Siebentritt, George Meyer, Gerald Boyd, Dave Bensen, Wayne Blanchard and Bill Chipman of the Federal Emergency Management Agency who throughout the preparation of this document have been most generous with their advice, constructive criticism, and support.

FOREWORD

Civil Defense--a dirty word? Civil Defense--war mongering? Civil Defense--anti-nuclear? Civil Defense--a waste of money? Civil Defense--the ultimate futility? What?

In my experience there is a relatively small fraction of our people who embrace some or all of those arguments. Many of them firmly believe that any kind of defense, civil or military, somehow increases the likelihood of war.

I have found no effective way to counter these extreme beliefs. In fact, I no longer try to argue these points other than supplying the facts. I am becoming increasingly convinced that the basic problem centers about the overall ignorance of the general public coupled with an overwhelming deluge of mis-information about some of the simplest facts about Civil Defense. Actually, it is a combination of mis-information and dis-information, most of which is disseminated through our collective media--newspapers, radio, TV and household magazines.

Unfortunately, most of the public's information comes through those media which are necessarily highly competitive businesses and must make a profit to survive. By their own admissions, unexciting news is no news, and the often dull and technical discussions associated with Civil Defense make unattractive copy, so they tend to develop and emphasize, often out of context, any unusual, exciting or dramatic tidbits that come to hand, no matter what the source. These soon become catchwords in conversations and it is truly amazing how many quickly mount the ladder into full-fledged "facts." Even when the right questions are asked, wrong answers are the ones likely to be given, whether through avarice or malice or ignorance. It takes real effort to dig out the real facts.

A principal purpose of this report has been to collect some of the more commonly heard questions and to provide informed answers to them. This has been accomplished by tapping the knowledge of many scientists, and others, who have had extensive personal experience with problems directly associated with Civil Defense.

These questions and answers will have little impact if they are allowed to remain buried. It is important that the readers of this document, especially the Health Physicists, take them to heart and use every opportunity to discuss them wherever they can find an audience.

Over the last three and one-half decades, my travels, both personal and official, have brought me into contact with large numbers of people from many walks of life. When my connection with radiation matters is exposed, the conversation frequently leads to Civil Defense. I was surprised to learn how many are deeply concerned that not enough is being done in this country about Civil Defense. There was almost a feeling of relief when I told them a little about what is being done but is not coming through the media to them. I have rarely found these listeners supporting the pronouncements of the professional naysayers.

And my final personal message:

No one wants any kind of war, especially a nuclear war, but until we possess greater assurances than we have today, it is sheer folly to bury our heads in the sand and just hope it won't happen. Arguments that Civil Defense actions would encourage (or discourage) any enemy who wills to attack us just don't make any sense.

The worst nuclear war that can be conceived today could leave in this country perhaps fifty million survivors. Sometimes people say, "I'd rather die in the first attack than live in the world that follows." Be that as it may, the survivors would not have the luxury of that choice. They could be in desperate straits, but history tells us most would follow their strong natural instincts for survival and would make every effort to continue to live. Clearly whatever the level of preparation made before an attack, it could only serve to improve, not worsen, the lot of the survivors.

Now it is up to you.

Lauriston S. Taylor

CONTENTS

Note: The names of the individuals who have responded to the questions appearing in this document are listed below in alphabetical order. Following each name is general subject identification. This in turn is followed by a summary of the topics covered. **BIOGRAPHICAL SKETCHES** for the respondents start on page 61. A comprehensive **SUBJECT INDEX** begins on page 77.

PREFACE	iii
ACKNOWLEDGEMENTS	v
FOREWORD	vii
LIST OF TABLES	xv

QUESTIONS AND RESPONSES

Lee Battes: Fallout from overseas nuclear detonations — 1

Mr. Battes' topics include the nature of the fallout from an overseas nuclear detonation, how it would differ from the fallout produced by an attack on this country, how serious the levels might be, the role of the Federal government in dealing with the hazard, and what could be done to minimize the health effects.

John Billheimer: Population relocation — 2

Dr. Billheimer considers the feasibility of emergency population-relocation and examines problems of caring for evacuees after their relocation.

Edward Bramlitt: Alpha radiation — 4

Dr. Bramlitt explains how nuclear weapons produce alpha radiation, its biological effects, and the degree and significance of the alpha hazard under differing attack conditions. He concludes with an overall assessment of the alpha radiation hazard in a nuclear attack.

Charles Bridgman and Arthur Hopkins: Predicting fallout radiation levels — 9

Dr. Bridgman and Major Hopkins present an overview of requirements to be met for a realistic prediction of radioactive fallout. One of the key factors--the mass of fallout material associated with various quantities of radioactive fallout--is examined in some detail.

Conrad Chester: Nuclear power reactors as potential targets — 12

Dr. Chester's discussion covers attractiveness of reactors as potential targets, their vulnerability, consequences of a direct or nearby hit, the relative contribution of reactor fission products, and means of enhancing survivability.

Roger Cloutier: Emergency use of radiochemical laboratory equipment   14

    Mr. Cloutier looks at the potential availability and utility of radiochemical laboratory equipment following nuclear attack. Possible difficulties in operating the equipment are discussed.

Martin Cohen: Naturally occurring fallout protection   14

    Dr. Cohen provides estimates about naturally occurring fallout radiation protection attributable to factors of the environment including such things as nearby structures, hills, trees and lakes. Weathering factors, such as rain and winds, also are considered.

D. A. Crossley, Jr.: Insects and nuclear war   15

    Dr. Crossley provided the material that suggested the first part of the title of this document, "Would the Insects Inherit the Earth?"

L. Wayne Davis: Mean lethal dose   16

    Mr. Davis discusses the current state of knowledge on levels of prompt radiation that are lethal within a few weeks after exposure.

Philip Dolan: The home-made atomic bomb   17

    Mr. Dolan identifies difficulties in fabricating a "home-made" atomic bomb and considers how developing technology may in the future reduce such difficulties.

Robert Ehrlich: Nuclear winter   21

    Dr. Ehrlich examines the "nuclear winter" hypothesis in terms of the uncertainties involved, whether the concept of a threshold-size attack makes sense and the impact of the hypotheses on the need for Civil Defense.

Russell Gates: EMP   23

    Mr. Gates looks at Electromagnetic Pulse (EMP) effects and the means of protecting against them.

Leon Gouré: Soviet Civil Defense   23

    Dr. Gouré discusses the contrasts between Soviet and American views about Civil Defense, and the nature of the Soviet Civil Defense program. He speculates about probable Soviet reactions if the United States were to step up its Civil Defense program.

Jack Greene: Fallout factors, attack warning times and "salted" weapons 27

Mr. Greene shows how to estimate levels of attack-produced fallout radiation and discusses its geographical distribution and how it reduces with time. He describes the expected biological effects of various radiation exposures and explains the concept of radiation protection in terms of protection factor (PF). Questions about a cobalt bomb and about possible attack warning times are addressed.

Sumner Griffin: Fallout effects on livestock 33

Dr. Griffin discusses the importance of and the means of achieving fallout protection for livestock. He comments on the relative safety of the meat from irradiated animals.

Stanley Kronenberg: Army radiation monitoring equipment 34

Dr. Kronenberg contrasts civilian and military needs for radiological instruments. He identifies scheduled additions to the Army inventory and comments on future prospects for a low-cost, all-purpose radiation monitoring device.

Edward Lessard: Fallout experience in the Marshall Islands 37

Mr. Lessard considers the effects of radioactive contamination resulting from the detonations of test shots in the Marshall Islands in terms of the lessons that might apply to a post-attack United States.

Howard Maccabee: The will to live 40

Dr. Maccabee questions the idea that people surviving a nuclear attack might not have the will to continue living.

Stanley Martin: Nuclear attack-produced fires 40

Mr. Martin addresses the problems of protecting personnel in areas subjected to mass fires. He talks about the possible influence of such fires on radioactive fallout deposition and distribution.

Fred Mettler, Jr.: The human immune response 41

Dr. Mettler's subject concerns how much and for how long fallout radiation exposures might affect the human immune system.

Jiri Nehnevajsa: Public attitudes about Civil Defense 43

Dr. Nehnevajsa summarizes years of public opinion research, including numerous polls investigating the American public's view of Civil Defense. He speculates about probable public reaction to the "nuclear winter" hypothesis.

Hillyer Norment: Fallout prediction computer models 46

> Dr. Norment identifies limitations and attributes of current fallout prediction models and comments on the probable influence of different fallout particle size distributions resulting from detonations over different types of soils.

Warren Sinclair: Cancer incidence in a post nuclear attack society 47

> Dr. Sinclair provides a basis for estimating the cancer effects of radiation exposures and contrasts the post-attack cancer death rates expected from different radiation exposures with the death rates due to cigarette smoking in today's society.

George Sisson: Fallout protection 48

> Mr. Sisson considers two types of fallout radiation protection: one relates to the protection to be found in mines and caves; and the other relates to fallout protected space that readily can be incorporated in new construction.

Paul Skierkowski: Protection against radioiodine 50

> Dr. Skierkowski examines the advantages and disadvantages of a program that in the event of a nuclear attack relies on administering stable iodine as a thyroid protective agent.

Kenneth Skrable: The neutron bomb 51

> Dr. Skrable describes the neutron bomb and how it might be employed in a wartime situation.

Richard Small: Asphyxiation 52

> Dr. Small considers the question about potential depletion of oxygen in shelters in large fire areas.

Lewis Spencer: The National Council on Radiation Protection and Measurements 52

> Dr. Spencer explains the role in Civil Defense planning of Scientific Committee 63 of the NCRP.

Daniel Strom: Carcinogenic and genetic effects of radiation exposures 53

> Dr. Strom reports on the incidence of cancer among workers in the nuclear weapons production industry, and looks at the genetic damage that could be produced in a nuclear war.

Walmer Strope: Civil Defense research 56

> Mr. Strope outlines the research base for Civil Defense programs.

Edward Teller: Ozone   58

    Dr. Teller explains the "ozone depletion" problem in the nuclear war context.

John Umbarger: The all-purpose radiation instrument   59

    Dr. Umbarger, from the point of view of an instrument scientist at Los Alamos, looks at problems and prospects of developing an inexpensive all-purpose wrist-watch-sized radiation meter.

Thomas Waterman: Protection in mass fire areas   59

    Mr. Waterman reports on research about protection of personnel from heat and noxious gases in mass fire areas.

Hubert Wilson: The all-purpose radiation instrument   60

    Mr. Wilson, from the point of view of an instrument scientist at the Oak Ridge National Laboratory, looks at problems and prospects of developing an inexpensive all-purpose wrist-watch-sized radiation meter.

BIOGRAPHICAL SKETCHES OF RESPONDENTS   61

GLOSSARY   71

REFERENCES   73

SUBJECT INDEX   77

LIST OF TABLES

Table A.	Significance of Alpha-Emitters in Various Scenarios	6
Table B.	Calculated Distribution of Dose Rates and Doses Over the U.S.	28
Table C.	Percentage of U.S. Land Areas Subjected to Various Dose-Rate Ranges at Various Times After the Assumed Attack	29
Table D.	Recommended System for Predicting Outcome of Gamma Radiation Exposure (the "Penalty" Table)	30
Table E.	Dosimetric Conclusions for the Protracted Exposure of Rongelap and Utirik Adults from Day of Return to 50 Years	39
Table F.	Perceived Reasons for Civil Defense	44
Table G.	Radiation Risk Coefficients (Fatal Cancers per Million Person-Rems)	55
Table H.	Expected Cancer Rates in U.S. Worker Populations	55
Table I.	Civil Defense Research Obligations, 1962-1971	57

QUESTIONS AND RESPONSES

What are the radiation hazards to be expected in the United States in the event of nuclear war (minor or major) between two overseas adversaries, say China and the Soviet Union? *(Respondent: Lee T. Battes)*

Overseas hostilities involving the large-scale use of nuclear weapons would probably result in the atmospheric transport and deposition of radioactive fallout in the United States, particularly in areas where rain or snow brings it to earth. While not expected to be life-threatening in the immediate sense, fallout would likely produce some long-term health effects which could be reduced through appropriate protective actions. Subsequent questions and answers provide further information on the subject.

What role would the federal government play in monitoring and protective actions? *(Respondent: Lee T. Battes)*

The Federal agencies involved are the Environmental Protection Agency (EPA), the Nuclear Regulatory Commission (NRC), the Department of Energy (DOE), the Food and Drug Administration (FDA), the Federal Aviation Administration (FAA), the National Oceanic and Atmospheric Administration (NOAA), the United States Air Force, and the Federal Emergency Management Agency (FEMA).

The EPA has the prime responsibility for advising the general public on the potential health significance of radioactive contamination. In this role, EPA is responsible for coordination of all Federal activities for public health protection and dissemination of information to the public. The FDA also has a major responsibility in the area of assuring that foods (exclusive of water for domestic consumption) are safe and wholesome. The EPA and the FDA will normally notify the State health agencies, who can provide additional guidance as needed to other State and local agencies.

DOE is responsible for making public announcements on the occurrence of nuclear detonations outside the U.S. The Air Force will provide data to other Federal agencies on airborne samples it collects. NOAA will provide official forecasts on the movement of airborne radioactivity and on areas of potential rainout of nuclear debris. NRC will provide to EPA any fallout data obtained from its licensees. FAA is responsible for the safety of air commerce. FEMA would provide coordination assistance and could activate Civil Defense radiological resources.

How does fallout from abroad differ from that caused by an attack on the United States? *(Respondent: Lee T. Battes)*

The fallout threat from an overseas nuclear conflict would differ in many important ways from that resulting from a large-scale attack on the United States. By the time fallout from overseas arrived here, its radioactivity would decay to well under one percent of the intensity one hour after detonation. Having reached this low level, however, its further decay would be quite slow, and could require several weeks to be reduced by an additional factor of 10.

If the United States were not itself attacked, the implementation of monitoring programs and protective actions could be organized through increased activation of existing government, industry and professional organizations.

In the event of a full-scale weapons exchange between the United States and another country, the most severe fallout would result from weapons detonated in this country, and the added fallout from detonations abroad would be relatively minor in comparison. In this case, immediate life-threatening radiation levels would be present in most of the United States, and protection of the public and resources could only be provided through the fully activated Civil Defense programs.

If weapons are detonated in the United States, the greatest fallout hazard is from near-surface explosions because of the mass of earth lifted by the fireball into the cloud, which soon returns to ground level downwind. For overseas detonations, air bursts generally result in a greater radiological threat because it is the smaller particles which are transported over large distances.

How serious would radiation levels be? *(Respondent: Lee T. Battes)*

Even a large-scale employment of nuclear weapons overseas would not result in a radiation hazard in the United States sufficient to cause radiation sickness. Exposure rates soon after deposition of fallout from overseas would probably be measured in hundredths of a roentgen per hour (R/hr), even in the more heavily contaminated areas. Total exposure over a period of about three months--assuming no countermeasures were taken--could range from about 1 R to as much as 10 R in heavily contaminated areas.

Factors which influence the degree of hazard include: total weapon yield; individual weapon size; design and proximity of detonation to the ground; type of soil at the detonation sites; prevailing wind direction and speed; and atmospheric scavenging through precipitation.

Generally speaking, ground radiation levels along the track of the airborne fallout plume will most heavily depend upon precipitation, and the West Coast is likely to be more at risk than the East Coast because of earlier arrival times resulting in less radioactive decay, atmospheric dispersion and opportunity for earlier ground deposition.

Although external exposures and inhalation doses are likely to be very low, the ingestion of contaminated milk and water could result in infant and child thyroid doses of several hundred rems.

What could be done to minimize health effects and how effective would such actions be? *(Respondent: Lee T. Battes)*

Since transport of fallout over the Pacific Ocean would take four or five days, there would be time to implement protective actions, even on the West Coast.

Protection of the thyroid from ingested radioactive iodine-131 (^{131}I), an abundant fission product with an 8-day half-life, could be achieved by placing dairy cattle on stored, uncontaminated feed and water. Activating milk monitoring programs would ensure quality control, and the use of canned or dried milk and milk-substitutes would be encouraged as necessary. Thyroid blocking with potassium iodide is not likely to be of much value since ingestion can be easily controlled.

Other agricultural produce may also be contaminated and advice on washing before eating would be provided. Some produce could be stored pending radioactive decay or diverted to use other than human consumption.

These countermeasures could readily reduce external (whole-body) exposure by about 90 percent, and internal organ exposures by about 90 to 99 percent. Some protective actions could be needed for a period of as much as three months.

Countermeasures against external exposure in areas of relatively heavy fallout deposition would include staying indoors for several weeks (longer for pregnant women and pre-school children). Decontamination of roofs and some areas around houses could also reduce exposures. Sheltering might reduce whole body exposure by 50 percent. In extreme cases, evacuation from very heavily contaminated areas would be considered.

Details on Chinese nuclear test assessments performed by EPA can be found in many issues of *Radiation Data and Reports* and by contacting the United States Environmental Protection Agency.

Do you believe that a Civil Defense strategy that calls for the evacuation of people from our larger cities in the event of a potential nuclear attack makes any sense? *(Respondent: John Billheimer)*

Absolutely. Given the existing scarcity of shelter space, there is no question that evacuation represents the best hope of protecting the residents of our larger cities. Eighty-five million of our country's citizens live in areas of over one million population. Successful evacuation procedures could save tens of millions of these lives in the event of a nuclear attack.

Past research has shown that United States cities generally have enough vehicles and fuel to support massive evacuations. In many large cities, however, road capacity is limited, so that careful planning and scheduling, along with continuous monitoring and control, will be needed to avoid severe traffic tie-ups. Evacuation of our largest cities cannot be done instantaneously. Large cities with ample outbound road capacity (e.g., Dallas, Atlanta) could be evacuated in less than a day by following pre-assigned routes. Larger cities bounded by water or other geographic barriers (e.g., Seattle, Detroit) are likely to require at least two days to clear. Our largest cities (e.g., New York, Chicago) will undoubtedly need at least three days to evacuate, even with advance planning.

No one knows how much time will be available to accomplish an evacuation. In the case of a true surprise attack, an evacuation strategy will have only a marginal value in our larger cities. Given any advance warning, however, evacuation can save many lives. Should global tensions increase, it is likely that some citizens will attempt to leave obvious target areas whether or not they are told to do so. In such an instance, it is essential that our largest cities have evacuation routes laid out in advance so that traffic jams do not develop on one or two routes while other exit routes are underutilized.

Large-scale evacuations have proven to be feasible in the face of hurricane warnings and accidents involving hazardous materials. Hurricane-threatened sections of large Gulf Coast cities have been cleared within ten hours of official evacuation orders. In November 1979, 217,000 residents of the Toronto suburb of Mississauga were evacuated within 24 hours of the derailment of a chlorine tanker.

There is no denying that a nuclear attack, with or without an evacuation, is an unmitigated catastrophe. But many more United States citizens can expect to survive such an attack if plans exist for their evacuation and protection.

What do you think are the most important actions that could be taken pre-attack to enhance the chances that people could successfully be evacuated and subsequently be provided for? *(Respondent: John Billheimer)*

It is absolutely essential that detailed plans assigning residents to evacuation routes be drawn up for our largest target areas. These plans should make optimum use of existing road capacity and address the need for scheduling departures and controlling traffic.

Plans for reallocating food following evacuation should be reviewed with individual distributors. The possibility of stockpiling processed food in reception areas should be investigated. Well-placed stockpiles would ensure a supply of food immediately following evacuation and reduce the vulnerability of the nation's food stocks if an attack occurs.

A public information program should be developed to counter the charges that evacuation plans are unrealistic, misleading, a questionable diversion of funds, or an escalation of the arms race. Groups that reject evacuation planning as a protest against the nuclear threat follow an absurd brand of logic. Such protests are the equivalent of cutting off seat belts to protest against drunk driving, or eliminating fire escapes because third-degree burns are too horrible to contemplate and the presence of a fire escape might encourage an arsonist. The misguided belief of disarmament advocates that Civil Defense represents an escalation of the arms race is currently blocking effective evacuation planning in many areas, and it could cost millions of lives if a nuclear attack should occur before disarmament goals are achieved.

Even if people could be successfully evacuated (whatever that means), do you think it would be possible to provide them with the basic necessities of life--especially food and water? *(Respondent: John Billheimer)*

The task of supporting an evacuated population, although it is by no means simple, is considerably less difficult than the evacuation itself. Extensive interviews with food industry representatives suggest that existing distribution channels are resilient and flexible enough to feed an evacuated population. Of the food stocks that would be immediately available at regional and local levels for distribution following an evacuation, wholesalers have between one and two weeks' supplies, and retail outlets have between one and two weeks' supplies, measured against current consumption levels. Consumers tend to maintain about one week's supply of food, and they could be expected to carry some food with them to reception areas.

Remember, under evacuation conditions, the food production and distribution system itself will have received no damage. The industry infrastructure that normally feeds the population will still be in place. Supply lines will be stretched, and provision must be made to protect workers who will continue to work in target areas to empty warehouses and keep essential production going. Roughly 85 percent of the nation's wholesale food stocks are stored in target areas. Industry leaders generally agree that the most effective strategy for distributing food to evacuees involves the continued operation of these warehouses, at least during the first few weeks following evacuation. The continued operation of these warehouses will place stress on the transportation lines linking target-area wholesalers with reception-area retailers and feeding centers. Much of this stress can be alleviated by eliminating non-essential shipments, improving equipment use and careful advance planning.

The food distribution system most likely to operate successfully following an evacuation is that system which closely resembles existing distribution channels. Distribution managers contacted to date, including representatives of such industry giants as Safeway, Kroger, and Fleming Foods, have been most cooperative in pledging support, reviewing plans, and offering suggestions for improving food distribution following an evacuation. The predominant reaction of industry leaders has been "just tell us where the people are, we'll get the food to them." Individual plans linking existing food distribution channels with region-wide evacuation patterns are currently being developed, and food industry leaders seem confident that food can be reallocated to support the evacuated population.

In the event of a nuclear attack on the United States, would alpha radiation emitters be a significant hazard? *(Respondent: Edward T. Bramlitt)*

Alpha emitters are associated with nuclear weapons, and they are hazardous if taken into the body in significant amounts. The adverse effects of alpha radiation occur long after intake, if at all. Alpha emitters will be one of the smallest hazards during the active phase of most postulated nuclear attacks, but they may represent the primary radiological hazard during some attacks where nuclear yields are few or none. Alpha emitters will be of long-term concern to survivors during post-attack recovery.

In what way do nuclear weapons provide a source of alpha radiation? *(Respondent: Edward T. Bramlitt)*

All nuclear weapons contain alpha emitters. The principal alpha emitters are the fissile nuclides, ^{235}U and ^{239}Pu. Nuclear weapons utilize large amounts of "depleted uranium" (essentially ^{238}U without any ^{235}U), which is a long-lived and fissionable alpha emitter. The ^{235}U and ^{238}U alpha emitters are insignificant from a radiological health point of view because of their extremely low specific activities--30,000 and 190,000 times smaller respectively than ^{239}Pu. Weapons-grade uranium does not have the radon daughters which cause natural uranium to be hazardous. The alpha emitters of interest with nuclear weapons are those of the transuranic elements which have shorter lifetimes than those of uranium.

"Plutonium" usually implies ^{239}Pu; however, weapons-grade plutonium is not ^{239}Pu only. ^{239}Pu is manufactured in nuclear reactors by neutron capture in ^{238}U. During the breeding process, some ^{239}Pu atoms capture neutrons to convert to ^{240}Pu, some ^{240}Pu atoms convert to ^{241}Pu, and so forth. Plutonium is chemically separated from the uranium source material, and it includes all plutonium isotopes produced, since they all have the same chemical properties.

^{240}Pu is a fissionable alpha emitter in those nuclear weapons which contain plutonium. ^{240}Pu can poison the fission chain reaction, so its abundance in weapons-grade plutonium is restricted. On an activity basis, weapons-grade plutonium may contain 20 percent ^{240}Pu. ^{241}Pu beta decays with a 13-year half-life to ^{241}Am, a long-lived and fissile alpha emitter. No ^{241}Am is present initially in chemically separated plutonium; however, ^{241}Am grows in as ^{241}Pu decays. ^{241}Am is expected to provide about five to fifteen percent of the alpha activity in a typical plutonium weapon, depending on the weapon age. For example, "plutonium" from a nuclear weapon mishap in 1962 was analyzed in 1980, and the ^{241}Am content amounted to 11.5 $\pm$ 3.8 percent of the total alpha activity. ^{239}Pu therefore provides about 65 to 75 percent of the alpha activity in plutonium weapons.

Nuclear weapon detonations yield alpha emitters. ^{239}Pu may be present as unconsumed nuclear fuel. Some weapons may be designed for efficient fuel consumption, especially if the supply of fissile material available to the weapon producer is limited. Others may be designed to enhance operational safety or weapon security, and they may leave unburned fuel after detonation. Various designs may also alter the division between fission and non-fission neutron captures. Multiple neutron captures in ^{238}U can substantially alter the residual mix of plutonium isotopes and introduce other transuranic element isotopes such as ^{242}Cm.

The composition of alpha emitters after a nuclear detonation may be much different from that in the original nuclear weapon. Post-detonation alpha emitter composition can be inferred from studies in the Marshall Islands, where atmospheric nuclear weapon tests (ANWT) were conducted between 1946 and 1958.

Environmental samples from Rongelap Atoll, which was contaminated primarily by fallout from one thermonuclear weapon test at Bikini Atoll in 1954, were analyzed in 1976 and found to have ^{241}Am making up about 30 percent of the total alpha activity. Many alpha activity analyses were made as part of the Enewetak Atoll radiological cleanup in 1977-1980. ^{241}Am ranged from about 20 to 40 percent of alpha activity at most of the islands subject to fallout from multiple nuclear tests. Samples from Bikini Atoll taken in 1970-1972 were found to have ^{241}Am at about 20 to 25 percent of total alpha activity. ^{241}Pu analyses indicate that ^{241}Am eventually will comprise about 50 percent of the alpha activity in the Marshall Islands. Following one large nuclear test at Enewetak Atoll in 1952, the amount of ^{241}Am was reported to be sufficient to eventually account for approximately 80 percent of total alpha activity.

Americium in the environment appears to be more chemically available for uptake by people than plutonium. In view of its abundance and its properties, ^{241}Am may be the primary alpha emitter of concern after a nuclear attack.

^{238}Pu is a relatively short-lived alpha emitter (88-year half-life) which can be produced by several paths, including (n,2n) reactions on ^{239}Pu. ^{238}Pu at Enewetak Atoll typically accounts for one to ten percent of total alpha activity, although samples associated with some tests showed ^{238}Pu to be in the range from 30 to 50 percent. Some studies indicate ^{238}Pu is more hazardous than ^{239}Pu, and this is attributed to the much higher specific activity for ^{238}Pu.

^{239}Pu and ^{240}Pu have almost identical radioactive decay properties, and most analyses of nuclear weapon debris report only the sum of activity for ^{239}Pu+^{240}Pu. The two isotopes can be differentiated by mass spectroscopy. Bikini and Enewetak samples analyzed in this manner show ^{240}Pu to account for 50 to 60 percent of combined ^{239}Pu+^{240}Pu activity.

Alpha activity from a nuclear weapon which fails to achieve nuclear yield, a dud, will be in approximately the same composition as in the original weapon fuel. Such an event occurred at Enewetak Atoll in 1958, and the ^{241}Am alpha activity was reported in 1972 to be about seven percent of the total alpha activity.

How does alpha radiation cause biological damage?
(Respondent: Edward T. Bramlitt)

The principal alpha emitters associated with nuclear weapons emit alpha particles with energies between 5.1 and 5.5 MeV. These particles have a range in air between 3.6 and 4.1 cm, and in tissue, about 35 micrometers (μm). The basal cell layer of the epidermis is considered the skin tissue most at risk since skin germinates there. Average epidermal thickness for head, trunk and upper extremities in adults is about 36 μm, and it is greater for other areas of the body. Alpha emitters from nuclear weapons are not a significant hazard if external to the body.

Alpha emitters are potentially hazardous if they enter the body since the surfaces of internal organs are sensitive tissues and alpha particles can deposit their energy in those tissues. Entry can occur through inhalation of air which is contaminated with depositing fallout or resuspended fallout; by ingestion of fallout-contaminated foods, liquids or soil; and by injection, as from puncture wounds with contaminated debris.

The inhalation pathway is generally considered the critical pathway for environmental transuranic element alpha emitters (TRU). Deposition of alpha emitters in the lungs depends on breathing rate and aerosol particle size. The physical half-life of the TRU may be considered infinite. The alpha emitters are expected to fit the lung clearance class "Y", which means a large percentage of material deposited in the lung will remain there for a long time. A 500-day biological half-life is normally assumed. The alpha sources can move from the lung to the gastrointestinal tract. Some will be absorbed through the tract walls into the blood and eventually be deposited on bone surfaces, where they remain indefinitely. ^{241}Am may be absorbed more readily than the plutonium alpha emitters.

Just how hazardous is alpha radiation?
(Respondent: Edward T. Bramlitt)

Transuranic element alpha emitters are considered the most toxic internal radionuclides. The maximum permissible lung burden for "radiation workers" historically has been set at 16 nanocuries (nCi); i.e., if 16 nCi are uniformly distributed in the lung and maintained at that level, a dose equivalent rate of 15 rem/yr will result. The maximum permissible concentration in air (MPC$_a$) which leads to this dose rate is 40 picocuries per cubic meter (pCi/m^3). Dose limits for members of the public are more stringent, and the MPC$_a$ has been 1 pCi/m^3. New metabolic models and a change in alpha particle quality factor from 10 to 20 may cause these permissible levels to be made more stringent by as much as a factor of 10.

The major health hazard from alpha emitters is indicated to be lung cancer. Excess deaths from lung cancers have been observed in studies of animals and people. An excess of neoplasms has been found in hamsters at 15 rads of alpha radiation and in a group of miners at cumulative dose to the bronchi of four to nine rads. A significant excess of lung cancers has been observed in a group of Hiroshima survivors who received 9.8 rads to the lung from gamma and neutron radiation and in a group of patients exposed to 197 rads of x radiation in increments of about 20 rads each. Death is not immediate; the latent period from radiation exposure to death from lung cancer in people is generally 10 or more years.

A 10 rad dose to lung of attack survivors might be considered indicative of harm; a 100 rad dose might be considered significant. A 100 rad dose will result from an acute intake of about 1.8 microcuries (μCi) of TRU whose average particle size is about 1 μm. (This intake would give a dose rate of 20 rads/yr in the first year after intake.) Likewise, 100 rads will result from chronic intake of about 120 pCi/d. (This gives a maximum dose rate to lung of two rad/yr after about six years of intake.) Air with these alpha emitters at 6 pCi/m^3 and breathed in the normal manner would cause such a chronic intake.

For peacetime purposes, the Environmental Protection Agency (EPA) has recommended limiting absorbed dose rate to lung of members of the general public from TRU to one millirad per year (mrad/yr). A large group of persons could receive doses at this rate continuously and the risk of excess lung cancer would be one in a million. Pathway dose analyses made by EPA indicate people can continuously inhale air with TRU at 1 femtocurie per cubic meter (fCi/m^3), or reside on soil contaminated to 0.2 µCi/m^2 at the ground surface, and the dose rate limit would not be exceeded. (The limits are based on an assumption that alpha emitters will be resuspended from the ground.) EPA termed these "safe" concentrations "screening levels." The soil screening level is equivalent to about 13 pCi/g in the top one cm of ground.

Under what nuclear attack conditions might alpha radiation be of concern? *(Respondent: Edward T. Bramlitt)*

A nuclear attack can have ground zeros (GZ) with nuclear bursts in the air or on the ground; there may be bursts with high nuclear yields, with low yields, or no yields; there may be fission products, induced activities, and alpha emitters; the concentrations of each radioisotope will vary in a different manner with time and location.

Radiological hazards cannot be isolated without consideration for other hazards, such as blasts, thermal radiation, the "nuclear winter," etc., and hazards from alpha emitters cannot be considered independent of those from other sources of radiation. Some generalizations must be made to consider the hazards of alpha emitters. Table A attempts this by classifying nuclear attack by affected environments as a function of time (during attack and post attack). A "no" means alpha emitters should not be significant, a "yes" means they may be significant. An example of the type of environment is also shown.

Radiological hazards from an air burst (Air GZ) will be from initial nuclear radiation (INR) neutrons and prompt gamma radiation emitted in the first minute following the nuclear burst. Casualties will result primarily from nonradiological weapon effects, except in the case of enhanced radiation weapons. (Such weapons are not expected to be used on the United States.) There will be some induced activity at the GZ location, but otherwise, there should be no long-lasting radiation. Many persons at Hiroshima and Nagasaki received INR doses, but persons who entered the cities after the attacks are reported to have received insignificant radiation doses. Alpha emitters can be disregarded during and after attacks in which there are only air bursts.

Alpha emitters will be of no concern during the attack where a surface GZ nuclear detonation occurs. This is not because alpha emitters are absent, but because other effects are predominant. Enewetak and Bikini Atolls may be considered typical of such target areas in a nuclear attack. Persons were evacuated from the vicinity of the target islands during the tests, but were returned shortly thereafter. The sites were used for testing on alternate years between 1946 and 1958 without concern over dose from residual radiation of previous tests. However, persons who took part in subsequent tests were classified as "occupationally exposed" and were authorized higher doses than are permitted for the general public; they did not consume locally grown food, and their occupancy was sufficiently short that doses from external exposure and inhalation were insignificant.

The residents of Bikini and Enewetak were relocated from their homes for over two decades because of residual radioactivity. A radiological cleanup of Bikini was accomplished in 1969. It involved removing contaminated debris (induced radioactivity and surface contamination) and hazardous non-contaminated debris and covering village areas with a layer of clean soil to reduce external radiation doses. Some restrictions were placed on the consumption of locally grown foods and use of some land. The goal was to maintain radiation doses below the current Federal levels permitted for the general public. The Bikini people gave up the resettlement effort in 1978,

---

Table A. **Significance of Alpha-Emitters in Various Scenarios.** Classifications are discussed in the text.

LOCATION	ATTACK	POST-ATTACK	EXAMPLE
Air GZ	No	No	Hiroshima/Nagasaki
Surface GZ	No	Yes	Enewetak/Bikini
Surface GZ --No Yield	Yes	Yes	Palomares/Thule
Early Fallout	No	Yes	Rongelap
Delayed Fallout	--	Yes	CONUS*

*Continental United States.

when bioassays indicated their uptake of residual ^{137}Cs was sufficient to cause dose limits to be exceeded if continued.

A radiological cleanup of Enewetak was accomplished in 1977-1980. The principal remaining radiological hazards were ^{60}Co, ^{137}Cs, ^{90}Sr and TRU. The TRU were limited primarily to the surface soil, whereas the ^{137}Cs and ^{90}Sr were distributed throughout due to their greater solubility. ^{60}Co was primarily associated with metal debris. Dose pathways in order of diminishing importance were ingestion of terrestrial food, ingestion of marine food, external exposure and inhalation of TRU. Dose from external exposure was made insignificant by removal of surface soil contaminated with TRU at levels greater than 40 pCi/g. Emphasis was given to removing alpha emitters, since given sufficient time (two or three generations), the remaining fission products would disappear through decay. A restricted lifestyle is required of the people who now live at Enewetak; however, all restrictions can be lifted in a few decades since alpha emitters have been removed. Based on these experiences, one might suspect that alpha emitters would be a concern to the long-term recovery of locations which suffer a surface GZ.

A surface GZ with no nuclear yield (a dud) could represent an alpha emitter hazard during and after the attack, but only to persons in the immediate vicinity of the GZ. There have been some nuclear weapon accidents, e.g., Palomares and Thule, which might approximate such an event, but people were not exposed during the accidents. The potential for doses from alpha emitters was present, and cleanups were performed. Duds are not expected to be significant in a nuclear attack, but they might pose isolated alpha-emitter hazards.

Fallout which occurs within the first 24 hours after a nuclear burst is "early fallout." Persons at Rongelap Atoll were exposed to early fallout in 1954; they received excessive doses from fission product radioactivities but no indication of dose from alpha emitters. They were evacuated from their islands until 1957 due to residual fission products, and restrictions on their current lifestyle continue due to remaining radioactivities. ^{137}Cs and ^{90}Sr are present at concentrations similar to and up to ten times more than TRU in isolated locations. An eventual removal of TRU may be required. Alpha emitters can be significant in the eventual recovery of areas subject to early fallout as evidenced at Rongelap.

Delayed fallout, or world-wide fallout, is that which is deposited more than 24 hours after detonation. Delayed fallout can be of concern only to post-attack survivability and recovery, since it occurs after the attack (assuming no protracted attack). It can provide an approximately uniformly distributed source of radiation and add to the levels of early fallout. The EPA has reported that approximately 430 kCi of plutonium were produced during the Atmospheric Nuclear Weapons Tests (ANWT): 105 kCi was deposited as early fallout; 325 kCi was injected to the stratosphere; and of this, 250 kCi was deposited in the middle latitudes of the northern hemisphere. There have been about 367 ANWT (212 by the United States, 134 by the U.S.S.R. and 21 by the United Kingdom). If the average quantity of plutonium in these tests was 10 kg, then there was about 230 kCi of plutonium employed, which suggests that about two times more plutonium was produced than was consumed.

A theoretical nuclear attack is proposed which involves 25,000 nuclear warheads with 10 kg weapons-grade plutonium each. By comparison with the ANWT, the 250,000 kg used would produce about 500,000 kg of alpha emitters. This amounts to about 150,000 kCi, if the average alpha emitter half-life is 5,000 years. If deposition were similar to ANWT, then about 86,000 kCi would deposit at middle latitudes. Furthermore, the integrated TRU concentrations in surface air in the United States from the ANWT is on the order of a few fCi/m^3, and the cumulative depositions of TRU on the ground surfaces in the United States ranged from one to three nanocuries per square meter (nCi/m^2). Delayed fallout from the assumed attack might increase levels some 340 times over the levels from ANWT. Air concentrations might be 1 pCi/m^3 and soil might reach 1 µCi/m^2. The air concentration would be one thousand times greater than the EPA air "screening level," but on the order of the MPC$_a$ (maximum permissible concentration in air) for members of the general public. The soil concentration would be about a factor of five greater than the EPA soil "screening level." Alpha emitters in delayed fallout would be a cause for some dose increase and would need to be considered along with other dose pathways; however, the resulting dose is not by itself sufficiently large to cause a significant dose increase.

A nuclear attack might have no nuclear detonations but cause widespread contamination with alpha emitters. In the spring of 1983, President Reagan announced a long-range program to protect the public from the threat of nuclear attack. The announcement was popularly dubbed the "star wars" speech and the effort was later officially titled the "Strategic Defense Initiative." The concept is to develop the means for shielding the nation from nuclear attack by destroying any incoming missiles and warheads before they detonate in the United States. "Far-out" ideas which have been mentioned include the use of satellites with lasers and antimatter beams capable of intercepting and destroying missiles shortly after their launch. Such methods might destroy warheads, but they could not destroy the nuclear fuel. If destruction occurs in the stratosphere, then the nuclear fuel would eventually filter down to the ground, like world-wide fallout from ANWT. Alternatively, the warheads might be disabled, yet continue their ballistic trajectory and cause the alpha emitters to be released at impact on the ground. A completely successful strategic defense of a large nuclear attack could cause a release of the attacker's entire inventory of alpha emitters. Such a scenario is considered below.

A theoretical nuclear attack is proposed which involves 25,000 nuclear warheads with 10 kg weapons-grade plutonium each as before. However, the warheads are assumed to be destroyed in one instance in the stratosphere and in another instance on the ground. The 250,000 kg of plutonium expended in this attack is approximately 16,000 kCi.

The attack impact for stratospheric injection is also estimated from ANWT results. ANWT were frequent until 1958 when they were terminated by mutual U.S.-U.S.S.R. agreement. Testing was unexpectedly resumed by the U.S.S.R. in 1961, and became extensive by both the U.S. and U.S.S.R. until a nuclear test ban treaty was adopted in 1963. The concentration of ^{239}Pu in air has been tracked at several locations. Data for New York City is considered typical. It shows the concentration of ^{239}Pu in surface air gradually increased from about 0.1 fCi/m^3 in 1954 to a peak of 0.45 fCi/m^3 in 1959, the year following completion of a large series of tests in the Pacific by the United States. The concentration decreased to about 0.1 fCi/m^3 in 1960 and 1961, and then it went through a much larger peak in the years 1962 through 1966, with annual concentrations being 0.63, 1.68, 0.91, 0.33 and 0.13 fCi/m^3, respectively. The net peak ^{239}Pu concentration in 1963 from the 1962 ANWT was thus about 1.6 fCi/m^3.

Ground depositions of ^{239}Pu in New York City were about 0.2 nCi/m^2 in 1959 and about 0.6 nCi/m^2 in 1963. Based on this, an assumption that three-fourths of the total stratospheric inventory (325 kCi) was injected in 1962 seems reasonable. Thus, about 245 kCi in the stratosphere caused a net increase of 1.6 fCi/m^3 in surface air. The theoretical attack which releases 16,000 kCi then might cause a peak concentration of about 100 fCi/m^3 in the year following the attack. Elevated levels might persist for many years, since decay of the 1962 ANWT plutonium-in-air peak was about three times longer than the 1958 ANWT peak.

Annual ground deposition in New York City for the years 1962 through 1966 also went through a peak, and the total deposition was about 1.5 nCi/m^2. If this was due to stratospheric fallout from 245 kCi, then the theoretical attack might cause ground contamination levels about 100 nCi/m^2 or about 0.1 µCi/m^2.

The EPA air and soil "screening levels" of 1 fCi/m^3 and 0.2 µCi/m^2, respectively, were conservatively based. If we assume they produce a lung dose rate of 1 mrad/yr, then the theoretical attack might cause the average person to receive a lung dose in the years immediately following the attack of 100 mrad/yr as a result of direct inhalation of contaminated air. This dose rate would be reached in the sixth year following initiation of intake and continue for as many years as the elevated concentration persisted. Using a quality factor of 20 for alpha particles, the lung dose rate would be equivalent to 2 rem/yr. Dose from resuspension of deposited alpha emitters would be in compliance with EPA guidelines and would not exceed 1 mrad/yr to the lung (20 mrem/yr).

The attack impact for ground deposition of 16,000 kCi is estimated by comparison with accidents and incidents involving nuclear weapons. Two major nuclear weapon accidents occurred at Palomares, Spain, and Thule, Greenland, when aircraft carrying nuclear weapons crashed. A missile with nuclear warhead aborted on the launch pad at Johnston Island in 1962. Some "safety shots" were conducted at the Department of Energy Nevada Test Site to assess the impact of plutonium dispersal following a nuclear weapon accident. In each of these instances, plutonium was released as an aerosol cloud which drifted downwind from the point of release depositing plutonium along the cloud path. The cloud might have a significant plutonium concentration for a mile or so, and ground contamination might extend over 10 to 100 acres. The average area contaminated by the impact of a nuclear warhead might be a square mile. The attacked population presumably would be inside shelters as a result of "star wars" warnings which undoubtedly would be issued. Most of the population could be protected from the cloud of alpha emitters by closing shelter openings and using filtered air. The 25,000 warheads might contaminate 25,000 mi^2. This is a small area with respect to the 570,000 mi^2 covered by large cities (Standard Metropolitan Statistical

Areas), or the three-million square miles in the United States outside of large cities. There would be a monumental effort to recover the dispersed plutonium and make the environment free of plutonium, but there should be few or no fatalities due to alpha emitters from such an attack.

What would be the overall assessment of the alpha radiation hazard in a nuclear attack? *(Respondent: Edward T. Bramlitt)*

Alpha emitters should not represent a significant hazard during the active phase of a nuclear attack which produces multiple nuclear yields; however, they can be a significant hazard during the recovery from such attack if current radiation safety standards are maintained. In view of the widespread contamination from the attack, there might be a relaxing of standards. On the other hand, because so many survivors would have received significant dose commitments, there might be a call for more stringent standards.

Alpha emitters might be a hazard during and following a nuclear attack which is met by a successful strategic nuclear defense because the defense could produce widespread plutonium contamination. The alpha emitter hazards from the attack, however, would be limited to the isolated spots near weapon impacts on the ground. The attack would result in a major environmental contaminating event by current peacetime standards, but a blessing to the alternative of localized blast and thermal effects and widespread dispersal of fission-product beta/gamma emitters.

Do we have sufficient knowledge to realistically estimate the amount of fallout radioactivity (and consequently the radiation levels) to be expected following a nuclear attack on this country? *(Respondents: Charles J. Bridgman and Arthur T. Hopkins)*

If the winds are known at the time of burst and during the time just after the burst, then we are able to predict fairly well the location and intensity of fallout radioactivity. There are a few uncertainties other than the winds, but we are confident that these other uncertainties lie within known limits or bounds. In order to describe the uncertainties in our knowledge, fallout prediction may be divided into a series of calculated or measured events: (1) the amount of radioactivity produced, (2) the physical form and loading of the dust particles which carry this radioactivity, (3) the maximum altitude to which these particles are carried by the rising fireball, (4) the mechanics by which the particles fall to the ground, (5) the transport of the particles by winds during that fall and, (6) the radiation levels which result from the final ground deposition of the dust. We shall discuss these in order.

The amount of radioactivity produced is well known from years of experimental measurement with laboratory samples. *The Effects of Nuclear Weapons* ("ENW") lists the amount as 530 gamma megacuries per kiloton of fission, measured at one hour after the nuclear burst (Glasstone and Dolan, 1977). [A megacurie is 3.7×10^{16} emissions per second]. There is a nearly equal amount of beta radiation, but it is usually ignored in fallout calculations because of the weak penetrating power of the beta. These radioactive atoms are the result of the fission of uranium or plutonium atoms into two (rarely three) fragments which are isotopes of other elements in the periodic table. These new isotopes usually have an excess neutron number, and they decay by gamma and beta emission until a stable isotope is formed. This decay is the source of fallout radiation.

An example of such a decay chain is:

$^{90}Br \longrightarrow {}^{90}Kr \longrightarrow {}^{90}Rb \longrightarrow {}^{90}Sr \longrightarrow {}^{90}Y \longrightarrow {}^{90}Zr$ (stable)

ENW suggests that there are over 300 such isotopes produced with varying abundances (Glasstone and Dolan, 1977, p. 390). The abundances are measured chain by chain and vary from a fraction of a percent up to about six percent. The radioactivity from all of the fallout at any time is the sum of the decay rate of all the isotopes present at that time. Computer calculations are easily able to follow the decay and compute precisely the sum or total activity at any time. However, it has been found that this bulk decay is well approximated by the Way-Wigner equation which states that the activity, A(t), at time t after detonation, is given by

$$A(t) = A(1 \text{ hour}) \cdot t^{-1.2} \quad (t \text{ in hours}).$$

ENW shows the Way-Wigner approximation superimposed on a computer calculated result (Glasstone and Dolan, 1977, pp. 392-393).

Physical form and loading of the dust particles are also known from measurements made during the early atmospheric tests. In the case of a high altitude burst, a hundred or so kilograms of bomb (case, fuse, etc.) are vaporized in the nuclear explosion, and this vapor, together with the radioactive fission products, is lofted to higher altitudes as hot gases (a hot air balloon without a skin). As the mixture cools, it forms very fine particles with diameters much less than a micron

(10^{-6} meter or 0.001 millimeters). Particles this small fall extremely slowly under gravity, remaining at high altitudes until vertical air movements or rain deposit them on the ground. High altitude in the case of megaton nuclear explosions is above the tropopause (in the stratosphere). Sub-micron particles tend to circulate in the stratosphere for months or even years before they sift out into the troposphere where they can be transported to the ground by vertical air movements or rains. Eisenbud suggests the half-life for this removal is 6 to 12 months, depending on the latitude of the bursts (Eisenbud, 1973, p. 363). During this time the fallout is spread completely around the earth and thus becomes global fallout. The resulting world-wide population threat is a concern, but it should not result in death or even immediate injury because of the delay in reaching the ground, during which time the activity has decayed, and because of the dispersion of radioactive particles around the hemisphere. By our calculation, a strategic exchange in the Northern Hemisphere of 5,000 megatons of air bursts would result in a dose of 5 rads to each unsheltered person in the northern hemisphere *if the fine dust were evenly distributed over this hemisphere.* This 5 rad dose is the result of only global fallout. Persons within the local fallout fields from surface bursts will be exposed to much larger doses unless adequate protection measures are taken. A study by the National Research Council (Neir, 1975, p. 5) suggests that local hot spots, hundreds of kilometers in size, might have levels up to 30 times the evenly-distributed value.

In the case of sub-megaton air bursts, especially a few kiloton tactical yields, the particles formed are still much less than a micron, but they remain in the troposphere, and the fallout is immediately available to be downwardly transported by rain or vertical air mass movements. It is very difficult to predict such deposition except in probabilistic terms based on the probability of rain.

In the case of surface bursts, the picture changes dramatically because so much more material is entrained in the rising cloud. Surface soil, water, rock, coral or other matter is vaporized or blown into the rising fireball. It has been suggested that between 0.3 and 1.0 tons of such material are added into the fireball *per ton of yield*. Some of this is in the form of fist-sized rocks which quickly fall back to earth to form the lip and debris around the crater, but in addition, some considerable surface material is vaporized or finely pulverized and carried to high altitudes with the radioactive fission products. Again as the mixture cools, particles are formed by nucleation, condensation and agglomeration. The resulting solid particles have diameters tens to a hundred or more microns. They are larger than the particles resulting from an air burst because of the larger volume of material available in the cooling fireball. Particles with diameters in this range do fall with gravity in a predictable way and reach the ground in minutes to several hours. The bulk of surface burst particles reach the ground within 24 hours. Fallout which arrives this quickly is deposited immediately downwind of the burst and is known as local fallout. Local fallout can result in very high, lethal doses to unsheltered individuals.

The fission products are incorporated both in the interior of these solid particles and on their surfaces. The fraction of radioactivity in the volume versus that on the surface is important and is described as "fractionation." Fractionation depends on the yield, the carrier material and the nuclear fuel. Measurements and theory predict volume fractions from 0.5 to 0.9 (surface fractions 0.1 to 0.5) with a rough average of all cases examined at about 0.7 volume distributed. There is some evidence that fission products distributed throughout the volume decay at a rate different from $t^{-1.2}$. Varying rates from $t^{-1.1}$ to $t^{-1.4}$ have been suggested.

The altitude and extent of the cloud at the time it stops rising also affect the activity reaching the ground at any location and time. The term "stabilized cloud" is applied to the mixture of hot gases at the time it stops rising. This occurs about five to eight minutes after a megaton burst. *ENW* has a graph of the visible cloud top and bottom as a function of yield (Glasstone and Dolan, 1977, p. 32). The mass of radioactive particles from a surface burst tends to be slightly lower than the visible cloud (due to gravity forces on the newly formed particles before stabilization). A rule of thumb suggests that the center of the radioactive particle cloud lies approximately at the bottom of the visible cloud. More precise values are suggested by Bauer (Bauer, 1974). Bauer also suggests values for the vertical and horizontal dimensions of the cloud, including horizontal spreading with time. These dimensions are a measure of dispersion and thus affect the radiation dose on the ground at any location and time.

The fall rate of particles from a surface burst (diameters from a few to a few hundred microns) is believed to be well known. Fall rates can be computed by balancing the aerodynamic drag force on a particle of known size at any altitude with the opposing gravitational force. The calculation is described by Bridgman and Bigelow (Bridgman and Bigelow, 1982). Arthur T. Hopkins, working with Bridgman, has recently had great success in using these fall mechanics to predict the ashfall from the May 18, 1980, Mount St. Helens volcanic eruption (Hopkins and Bridgman, 1985). Gogolin has recently used these same fall mechanics to compute the rate of deposition (the integral of this rate is the fraction down) for a range of surface burst size distributions and fractionation ratios (Gogolin, 1984). The results vary from case to case, but not dramatically or widely.

The variability of the winds from the surface to the stratosphere and from point to point and time to time is the greatest uncertainty in our ability to predict where fallout will be deposited. Not only are vast amounts of wind data necessary but equally necessary is the ability to forecast wind changes as the fallout cloud moves and disperses. After-the-fact computations are possible on very large computers, but pre-attack calculations made months or years in advance are meaningless. What can be done is to make calculations with measured winds, day by day, and then predict fallout probabilistically based on the historic frequency of those winds occurring.

Finally, *the conversion from dose to death or injury* is discussed in *ENW* (Glasstone and Dolan, 1977, pp. 580-581). The results are again probabilistic because of uncertain measurement of dose in the case of Hiroshima-Nagasaki victims and in the few industrial accidents since that time. The usually-quoted values are that a dose of about 450 rad will result in a 50 percent chance of death within 30 days of exposure. A few deaths will occur at 200 rad, and nearly all will die at 700 rad.

In summary, we are confident about our ability to predict the total radiation produced, its physical form, its decay and its rate of deposition on the ground. We are not able to predict exactly where it lands on the ground because that is controlled by the winds and weather in the troposphere. We can, however, make statistical calculations based on past winds, and we can make bounding calculations for world-wide deposition.

What do we know about the mass of fallout material likely to be associated with various quantities of fallout radioactivity? *(Respondents: Charles J. Bridgman and Arthur T. Hopkins)*

The amount of fallout activity is 530 gamma megacuries per kiloton of fission yield at one hour after burst (Glasstone and Dolan, 1977, p. 453). The soil lofted in the case of a surface burst is quoted as 0.3 to 1 ton of soil per ton of yield. Much of this soil uplifted is in the form of rocks or boulders, but the rest is vaporized and pulverized and, upon condensation, becomes the dust which carries the fission fragment radioactivity.

The value 0.3 to 1 ton per ton is usually associated with a contact surface burst. Against super-hard silos, one targeting strategy which has been suggested is to employ very low altitude bursts to optimize the air slap on the silo. Such a burst may technically be a surface burst (x-ray fireball intersects the ground) but it should result in less soil lofted than 0.3 to 1 ton per ton. The less soil involved, the smaller will be the carrier particles, which means that the grounding of activity will be slower after the burst. This will result in greater doses downwind at the expense of close-in doses. This could increase or decrease the population dose, depending on the population location.

Earth penetrator warheads have also been suggested. A partially buried burst will loft less dirt *and less radioactivity*. There will be less radioactivity because some will be trapped in the ground around the detonation point. However, the carrier particle sizes might be larger, so the radioactivity will land sooner than would be the case for a contact surface burst. This may increase or decrease the population dose for the same reason cited above.

What do we know about particle size distributions from fallout that would be created by nuclear explosives over cities or soils different from the desert or coral of the Nevada and Pacific tests sites? *(Respondents: Charles J. Bridgman and Arthur T. Hopkins)*

The particle size distributions from the pre-1964 tests have been well examined and reported. Most researchers fit them with a lognormal distribution. A summary of four such distributions is given by Bigelow (Bigelow, 1983). These four include the smallest and largest which have been reported for surface bursts and two in between. When these distributions are transformed into mass radius distributions, their median radii vary from 50 microns (low yield over desert) to 200 microns (high yields over coral). The two "in between" distributions have median radii of 65 and 68 microns. Thus, there is surprising agreement in the sizes of these particles from very different soils. Further, when their sizes are compared to volcanic ash fall, Mt. St. Helens in particular, we find the same range of sizes, mass medians from 29 to 315 microns (Fruchter et al., 1980).

There are two uncertainties concerning the above data. First, the number of very small, sub-micron, particles is suspect because of our ability to collect and count such particles, even under a microscope. For this reason, some researchers prefer a power law distribution rather than a lognormal distribution. The power law predicts ever-increasing numbers of smaller particles down to some cut-off radius. This uncertainty, however, is not important, because very small particles carry a vanishingly small fraction of the total mass or of the total radioactivity. Further, the fall mechanics of such very small particles are controlled by vertical air movements--not by the force of gravity acting on their mass. The second uncertainty concerns the possibility of agglomeration and subsequent break-up when the fallen particles are sized by sieving. The agitation inherent in handling and sieving may break up particles which fell as larger agglomerations. There is some evidence from the Mt. St. Helens ash fall that this did in fact occur, so that the fallen (measured) size distributions are smaller than the falling distribution. This may also be true of nuclear fallout.

How attractive do you think U.S. power reactors would be to Soviet targeteers if we should get into a nuclear war with the Soviet Union?
(Respondent: Conrad V. Chester)

Power reactors must be considered strategic targets. A thousand megawatt reactor produces three kilograms of plutonium per day, and can be a source of nuclear material for weapons if properly operated and if the reprocessing facilities are available. Soviet strategic writers have, on more than one occasion, referred to the elimination of a nation's nuclear weapons-producing capability as one of the strategic objectives in a nuclear war.

In addition, nuclear power reactors can produce large amounts of electricity in a post-attack environment for months or years without making any demands on coal production or the transportation system. They are extremely valuable recovery assets. We must, therefore, assume they will be targeted, even though they are in remote locations.

How difficult would it be to destroy a typical United States power reactor?
(Respondent: Conrad V. Chester)

Most military targeteers are impressed by the massive steel and concrete construction of reactor containment buildings and thus assume that reactors are extremely hard targets which require a surface or low air burst.

Nuclear power plants can be put out of operation with relatively low overpressures. The most vulnerable structures are the cooling towers which will suffer catastrophic damage at one or two pounds per square inch (psi). At about three psi or a little over, transmission towers will fail, due to drag from the blast wind if it is at right angles to the transmission line, as will the concrete supporting structure of hyperbolic natural convection cooling towers. At somewhat higher overpressures, some water tanks will be knocked over, as will some light auxiliary buildings. At around 25 psi, some installations will experience damage to the diesel auxiliary generators and some containment will be damaged. Depending upon construction, this overpressure may get into control rooms and cause catastrophic damage.

Most reactor installations will be irrevocably damaged at around 25 psi. If the reactor has been operating for any length of time, there will be enough fission product afterheat in the core to destroy the core some hours or days after the loss of cooling water. Destruction of the core with damaged containment and damaged safety systems will very likely result in the emission of aerosols of volatile and semi-volatile fission products, which will be lethal for a few miles downwind.

One exception is a reactor site in which the ground water table or river level is higher than the level of the pressure vessel in the containment, and the damage is such that an opening between either ground water or river water permits the lower part of the containment to flood. Very little aerosol will escape from a reactor vessel if its openings are below water. Extreme examples of this situation are the nuclear propulsion units of the submarines Thresher and Scorpion which were sunk in deep water in the Atlantic, and a Soviet nuclear submarine sunk in the Pacific.

What would happen if a nuclear power reactor sustained a direct hit or a nearby hit?
(Respondent: Conrad V. Chester)

If a megaton-range nuclear weapon lands within 100 or 200 feet of a reactor, the pressure vessel can be ruptured and the core broken up and added to the fallout. If the reactor is running at the time it is hit, an hour after detonation the activity of the reactor's fission products will be approximately one percent of the fission products from a typical megaton nuclear weapon, and as such, add nothing to the immediate fallout hazard. However, the fallout from a megaton weapon will be very severe one to five miles away, especially if downwind.

If the reactor is outside the crater and anywhere within the 25 psi circle, the protective systems will be destroyed and the reactor will undergo an uncontained melt-down. If the containment rubble is not underwater, the volatile and semi-volatile fission products, such as cesium, ruthenium, and iodine, will be cooked out of the core hours after the stem winds from the weapon have subsided. The resulting aerosol will present an inhalation hazard to people without respiratory protection up to a few miles downwind, depending very strongly on meteorological conditions. This threat will not be serious to people in shelters equipped with high-efficiency air filters (99.97 percent for 0.3 micron particles) and potassium iodide pills. Even without the filtration, the aerosol from the fission products will present a statistically small hazard to crews in shelters if they are located a few miles upwind in the prevailing wind, or in a direction which is very rarely downwind.

How would reactor fission products contribute to the radiation dose? *(Respondent: Conrad V. Chester)*

In order to add reactor fission products to fallout, the containment must be blown away and the pressure vessel must be split open, and the core rejected and broken into pieces small enough to be entrained by the stem winds of the nuclear explosion. To break open the pressure vessel requires an impulse to the exterior containment in the neighborhood of 200 psi-seconds. To comminute the core sufficiently for it to be airborne by the after winds, higher overpressures will be required. We are not sure how high, but we are reasonably confident that a burst essentially in contact with the outer containment shell will do the job. This accuracy is achieved today by current cruise missiles.

If the reactor core inventory is added to the weapon fallout, it will increase radiation levels one hour after the detonation by one percent in the case of a one megaton weapon or ten percent in the case of 100 kiloton weapon. I consider it very unlikely that a Soviet targeteer would attempt direct hits on all the reactors in a multiple reactor installation.

The principal consequence of adding reactor products to fallout would be observed at very long times after the attack. This is due to the much larger inventory of long-life fission products, notably strontium and cesium in a 1000 megawatt reactor core compared to a one megaton weapon. Incorporation of a 1000 megawatt core in a megaton fallout field would increase the residual activity a year after the attack by about a factor of 8. However, this would present a health hazard only in the relatively small area around the point of detonation.

What plans could be made to enhance the survivability of nuclear reactors that are not hit directly? *(Respondent: Conrad V. Chester)*

A policy for reactor operations during a crisis relocation should have two objectives: to minimize the danger to the lives of the crew; and to prevent damage to reactors which are not struck by nuclear weapons.

In a crisis relocation, one would expect a big reduction in demand for electric power nationwide. Large parts of the economy would shut down as people moved from all-electric luxury to austere living conditions in the host areas. It would be well to take nuclear plants off the line with this reduction in load since they require fewer people on standby when they are shut down, and they are much more damage-tolerant.

Since reactors are likely to be strategic targets, crew requirements would be reduced if they were put on safe shutdown, as would the danger of the reactor damaging itself due to malfunction or minor damage. On-duty crews must have access to a competent blast shelter a safe distance from the reactor. Procedures should be developed to maximize the time the shutdown reactor can be left unattended.

When shut down, the reactors still require operation of the pumps and the residual heat-removal systems to continue to cool the core from fission product afterheat. This will require line electric power or operation of the auxiliary diesel generators. The line power can be expected to disappear at the moment of attack. The national grid can be expected to go down due to electromagnetic pulse, or unbalanced losses of load and generators even if not sustaining other damage. The auxiliary diesel generators will switch on automatically and, in theory, maintain the reactor in a safe condition for as long as the diesel fuel lasts. Many reactors have a seven-day supply.

As the core cools down and the decay power drops, at some point it will be possible to rely on natural convection in the reactor to cool the core, if there is a heat sink in the system. By this and other techniques, the amount of electric power to keep the reactor in a safe condition can be greatly reduced, and the diesel fuel supply correspondingly extended.

These remarks apply if power from the reactor is not needed by critical industries. If the critical industry in the grid cannot be supplied by other sources, then the reactor should be kept on line. The incremental improvement in the survival chances of the reactor and crew added by reactor shutdown is much less valuable than keeping critical industry operating.

Emergency crews manning the reactor during the crisis must be equipped with good blast shelter, preferably 50 psi or better, at least one mile from the reactor, and five miles would be preferable. I assume there will be some system giving them ten or fifteen minutes tactical warning, and that they will have some type of automotive transportation.

Will laboratory radiation-measuring equipment be useful in the post-nuclear attack period? *(Respondent: Roger J. Cloutier)*

Yes. Nuclear war will result in widespread distribution of radioactive fallout. Trained radiation monitors using Civil Defense radiation monitoring equipment will be able to measure the distribution of the fallout and the intensity of the radiation levels. Specialized radiation measuring equipment will also be available, for such equipment is already located throughout the United States at government and non-governmental laboratories. Because this equipment is routinely used for educational, medical, and industrial purposes, it is in regular use by skilled workers. The data generated by these groups can be used to inform the sheltered population about the types of radiations to be encountered and how to further improve radiation protection conditions. These data will also provide the population with the information they need before leaving the shelter to initiate the recovery process.

Because the laboratory equipment is more sophisticated than the Civil Defense instrumentation, it can be used to identify the individual nuclides present in the fallout. This information allows future radiation levels to be predicted more accurately than can be done with Civil Defense instruments. Because the laboratory equipment identifies individual nuclides, these data can also be used to predict the risk of internal exposure. Tens of thousands of simple NaI gamma-ray spectroscopy systems and more than 2,500 germanium type detectors are in use in the U.S. If these instruments were uniformly spaced throughout the United States, there would be an instrument within 50 miles of each other; however, the distribution of laboratory equipment is essentially the same as the population distribution.

Although germanium detectors operate at a cryogenic temperature by using liquid nitrogen, this is not considered to be a serious problem because most laboratories maintain a sufficient liquid nitrogen supply to last two weeks or more, and supplies of liquid nitrogen can probably be replenished even after a nuclear war. Even if the supply of liquid nitrogen were to be expended after two weeks, measurements could still be made with the NaI detectors. Although the NaI energy resolution (ability to identify radionuclides) is not as good as the germanium detectors, these detectors would be capable of handling the fallout problem after two weeks, when many of the radionuclides would have decayed and energy resolution requirements would no longer be so restrictive.

This availability of laboratory radiation-measuring equipment can greatly assist in the assessment of the post-nuclear war environment and help to save lives.

What are the factors contributing to reduction in fallout exposures in urban areas compared to the smooth, semi-infinite plane model? *(Respondent: Martin O. Cohen)*

The results of many years of experiments and calculations are available to help planners assess the gamma radiation exposures which might be experienced by people in an urban environment subjected to fallout from nuclear explosions.

The overall results indicate that rather high protection factors (PF) may be achieved. For example, for an isolated multi-story concrete building surrounded by an assumed "infinite" uniform fallout field in the streets (and on the roof), PF's of 10 to 30 can be expected in rooms just under the roof or along outside walls (away from unblocked windows). Inner rooms would have PF's of 30 to 100 and basements would provide even higher values. As will be seen, these values are probably conservatively low.

The location of such a building (or any typical urban structure) in a true urban environment leads to a large number of possible geometric configurations due to the almost countless possibilities of building and street arrangements. Nevertheless, it can be concluded that most shielding estimates, such as the ones given above, are considerably conservative in a true urban environment. Even the few "odd-ball" situations, where urban and/or weathering effects might reduce the expected protection, would be more than compensated for by the many instances where even greater increases in protection would be anticipated.

First let us realize that most calculations and experiments are conservative to begin with. They are usually based on the assumption of an emitted gamma ray spectrum approximated by that of ^{60}Co (average energy of about 1.25 MeV). This corresponds roughly to the average fallout spectrum at time t + 1 hour. At later times, the energy spectrum is, in fact, much softer, and thus the gamma radiation is less likely to penetrate the urban structures. Increases in PF's by factors of up to 2 are not unusual.

The calculations also assume a smooth infinite fallout plane. No surface is perfectly smooth and any roughness serves to reduce radiation exposure. Furthermore, in urban situations much fallout is not on the streets but on the roofs of buildings, some of which are rather high. For a completely unprotected person on the streets, the net effect of having fallout on the roofs is that the dose levels are reduced and, typically, effective PF's of about 2 are already achieved (dropping to about 1.5 at intersections). By avoiding the center of the streets, the above value can be further increased to above 2.5 in typical situations. Should the action of weathering move most of the fallout to one side of the street, PF's of over 10 can be expected on the "safe" side of the street. Finally, should a complete washdown of a street occur, due to rain washing the fallout into sewers or due to decontamination hosedowns, leaving fallout only on the roofs, PF's of over 100 would be achieved.

Within the urban structures, the PF's could be expected to exceed the "ideal" values of a single person within an isolated home surrounded by a smooth plane. First, in an urban environment people may be crowded into selected rooms. Calculations for residential homes have shown that a group of people sitting back-to-back, and fairly close to each other, would provide a significant amount of "mutual shielding." This would increase the building PF's by multiplicative factors varying between 1.5 and 3.

Second, the outside ground may not be smooth. In fact, in an urban environment which has suffered blast damage, wood and concrete debris may litter the streets -- especially in downtown areas. Calculations have shown that, per foot of debris (50 percent wood or concrete and 50 percent air, by volume), the shielding protection can rise by factors of 3 to 10 assuming that the fallout would be uniformly distributed (by weathering effects) amongst the debris. Even if the fallout rested on top of the debris, the irregularity of the surface would serve to reduce radiation exposures.

Third, even without debris in the streets, the distribution of fallout on the ground would not be uniform due to various weathering effects. Thus, the fallout would tend to pile up in some areas and be removed from others. As a result, some sheltered rooms would suffer while others would benefit. The availability of even the most unsophisticated radiation detectors could be used to lead people to areas which are safer than predicted.

Finally, the presence of nearby adjacent structures would provide significant mutual shielding between buildings. The possible situations are too numerous to assess here, but in all cases exposures within structures would be considerably below those predicted for buildings in isolation. Some studies have shown that additional multiplicative protection factors of 2 to 3 are quite reasonable to assume.

Would you care to speculate about the consequences to the insects if a nuclear attack on this country should occur, producing fairly high-level widespread radiological contamination? *(Respondent: D.A. Crossley, Jr.)*

Judging by other comments, this question is based on the premise that insect populations are really controlled by birds, which are much more radiosensitive than are insects. Thus, widespread contamination might reduce bird populations to the point that insects could increase unchecked. A large number of factors, biotic and abiotic, influence the size of insect populations. Birds are only one of them, and for many species of insects, birds are of little importance as determinants of population size. However, the question of insect population response to a thermonuclear war is still an interesting one.

First, some comments about insect sensitivity to ionizing radiation are appropriate. Insects lack the extremely radiosensitive systems of mammals and birds: for example, mucous membranes, replaceable epithelia, and hematopoietic systems. Thus, they can survive exposures to about 1000 R acute dosage without increased mortality (in fact, their longevity may increase slightly following exposures to 500-1000 R, which led one health physicist to propose that a little radiation is good for you). Insects may be sterilized by exposures to 1000-2000 R or so, depending on species, dose rate and other factors. Mortality effects appear after exposure to several thousand R, but they may require several days to be manifest (the "period of delayed response"). Sterility may account for the observed phenomenon of increased longevity. Species of insects vary largely in their sensitivity to radiation, however, and the sensitivity is related to species group, size, diet, and doubtless other factors. Life history phenomena may become altered, so that otherwise viable and fertile insects may not be able to mate.

It is not clear what regulates population size for most insect species, although a number of environmental factors may operate at one time or another. Scientists working in deserts are impressed with abiotic factors. Much of the argument for climatic control of insect populations comes from studies of desert species. Other studies argue for biological factors such as disease, parasitism or predation. Genetic deterioration may become important in large populations. Changes in quality of the food resource can lead to population growth or decline. The consequences of many of these biological factors are such that they can become more severe for large populations and less severe for small ones. Disease, for example, can be much more significant in large populations where the opportunity for transmission is higher. In the early 1900s, entomologists noted that birds really are not very likely to control insect populations. Insects can simply outbreed birds. Birds do eat lots of insects, and may learn to concentrate on species that are particularly numerous. However, effects of predation by birds generally do not become more important as insect populations get larger. Sooner or later, insects will "escape from control." For any given insect species, at any given time, various factors may cooperate to set population size.

Given these uncertainties about population regulation, what might be expected following nuclear contamination? Let us consider insect response to other types of catastrophes. Insects are opportunistic species, able to undergo rapid population growth following a catastrophe. The application of an insecticide, for example, is a catastrophe to the insect community. Frequently, insect populations recover and may grow rapidly to even higher population levels--the phenomenon known as resurgence. Different species may appear in large numbers, necessitating further applications of insecticides (the "pesticide treadmill"). Evidently what happens is that the insecticide reduces populations of predators and prey alike, but the herbivorous species can out-reproduce the carnivorous ones, and are therefore able to recover their population sizes much more rapidly. Naturally-occurring catastrophes--hurricanes, late freezes--may similarly induce insect outbreaks. Likewise, the sudden production of an abundant resource may have a catastrophic effect. If animal stockyards are flooded, there will be large outbreaks of flies, responding to the sudden availability of carrion. I have heard that there was an outbreak of houseflies following the bombing of Hiroshima.

Let us return to the original question, which proposed fairly widespread high-level contamination. If you are considering 5,000-10,000 R exposure to broad geographic areas, delivered fairly acutely, then you are talking lots of dead and/or sterile insects. But more realistically, there might be pockets of lower dosage. How much protection might be afforded by wet soil? Many insects might be hibernating deep in the soil, where they might receive lower doses. And even a few survivors might readily develop large population sizes, assuming their food resources survive also. Given the variability to be expected even in widespread contamination, it seems likely that insects would not only survive, but under some conditions would reach outbreak proportions.

What is the significance of this? Should we be stockpiling pesticides to fight off the onslaught of insects in the post-attack environment? Maybe so, but I can think of more important things to stockpile. If agriculture recovers sufficiently to produce a major harvest, then it would appear that our technological culture has survived. Fuel and fertilizer resources must have been available, and our distribution and communication systems must have remained intact. Under those circumstances, we probably would have normal control procedures in place. If the contamination was truly catastrophic, enough to engender a real insect outbreak, then we probably would have other things to worry about.

Ultimately, the "sage" may be correct. Cockroaches may be the final beneficiaries of all of our labor. They are able to feed on dead, decaying organic matter which we might produce in great supply. Cockroaches are fairly radiosensitive as insects go, however; I think I would put my money on one of the little fungus gnats or chironomid flies. Even given the "nuclear winter," the final observer of our stewardship of the earth may be a melancholy gnat.

Can the Japanese data provide a useful estimate of the mean lethal dose (MLD, or sometimes called LD-50) from initial nuclear radiation (INR), and what remains to be done? *(Respondent: L. Wayne Davis)*

I hope so. It can certainly narrow the range of estimates now being tossed about. However, I would not put much faith in any present estimates of the MLD which claim to be based on the Japanese data. The estimates are undoubtedly based on mortality curves which include both mechanical and thermal injuries, as well as radiation injuries. Thus, if one assumes, incorrectly, that the 50 percent mortality point (or range) is due entirely to the INR present at that range, then the dose thus calculated will be too low.

The 50 percent mortality point for people who were outside and unshielded occurred at a very low level of INR since the people died of flash burns.

The 50 percent mortality point for people in wood-frame dwellings occurred at a higher dose, still less than the MLD, because they received mostly mechanical injuries (from collapsing buildings), prompt-thermal injuries (if in front of windows), and also INR. (At the 5 psi level, where the structures were completely flattened, about ten percent of the people were killed.)

The theoretical INR mortality curves which we had calculated for the various shielding categories are quite compatible with all of the Japanese data and are based on a mean lethal dose of 450 rad in free air.

In order to obtain INR doses sufficiently high to justify a MLD of 450 rad free air, one must examine the casualty data in concrete buildings closer to ground zero. Dikewood (a research corporation in Albuquerque, NM) presently is examining cases of individuals who were shielded from flash burns and who received few mechanical injuries from the spalling concrete in the heavy buildings that survived the blast. The most difficult part of this analysis is to determine accurately the nuclear radiation shielding provided by the concrete in the building for each person at his precise location. This part of the study, only recently possible, is (early 1986) being performed at the Oak Ridge National Laboratory, utilizing a new state-of-the-art shielding code. Two of the Nagasaki buildings are being studied. We hope to have research results in the Spring of 1986 if funding remains available. (Other concrete buildings in both Hiroshima and Nagasaki could also be examined if the data currently being generated prove to be useful.)

It should be noted that the MLD for INR is not necessarily the same as the MLD for fallout radiation. Since the fallout radiation would be delivered at lower (perhaps much lower) dose rates than a MLD of INR, the human body possibly could repair some part of the radiation damage. Consequently, one would expect the MLD for fallout to be somewhat higher than the MLD for INR.

Do you think it is inevitable that sooner or later some terrorist organization will fabricate a perhaps crude but nevertheless workable nuclear device, and either seriously threaten its use or actually cause it to be detonated? *(Respondent: Philip Dolan)*

I will give a qualified yes in answer to the question. I think that it probably is inevitable that a nuclear device will be used by terrorists at some time in the future, either as a serious threat or with an actual explosion. The qualification arises from the fact that I believe that there is some probability that the acquisition may come about by theft of a weapon rather than by fabrication.

That is not to say that fabrication would be impossible. A great deal has been written about clandestine fabrication of nuclear weapons during the last decade. The topic has been the subject of novels, movies, and TV shows. General design principles have been described in the open literature by knowledgeable authors. Various student groups and other individuals have "designed" nuclear weapons, and the results of several of these efforts have been publicized. Many of these "designs" were of questionable effectiveness, but general principles were correct. In addition to the popular press, various unclassified journals and other technical publications contain such details as the chemical and metallurgical properties of plutonium and uranium. No doubt, there is enough information available in the open literature to enable a group to build a nuclear warhead.

Mass destruction weapons have become increasingly popular with terrorists during the last few years, and nuclear devices offer a relatively light and compact package for a specified destructive capability. Additionally, nuclear weapons could pose a significant threat without inflicting casualties. One has only to imagine the reaction within the United States if a low yield nuclear explosion took place in a desolate area, but in a location where detection and identification were certain. Then, if the explosion were followed by a terrorist claim of responsibility together with an announcement that three other devices were emplaced in three different cities, what would be the reaction to the inevitable demands that would accompany the announcement? What would be the reaction of Congress if the first explosion took place in the Blue Ridge mountains, and Washington,

D.C. were named, or guessed to be, one of the threatened cities? Nuclear weapons probably appear to be an attractive option to several terrorist groups.

There is an added factor that the terrorist who intends to explode a nuclear device only needs to ensure that he obtains a nuclear "bang", complete with the telltale mushroom cloud. Yield predictability is unimportant. The terrorist does not care whether he gets 10 kilotons of yield or 50 kilotons or even less than one kiloton. Toppling the Washington Monument or damaging the Capitol is adequate; Washington, D.C. and the surrounding suburbs need not be demolished. We must agree that a dedicated group could put together a possibly very inefficient device that would produce somewhere between a few tens of tons and a few kilotons of yield, which would be adequate for their purpose.

The question then becomes, how easy is it to construct a crude nuclear weapon? There are writers, who are themselves experienced warhead designers, who believe that any reasonably intelligent amateur could fabricate a workable device, but most experts hesitate to accept the premise that virtually anyone would have a certainty of success. No one who has seriously considered the problem would claim that the equipment and talent available at one of the U.S. National Laboratories would be required to design and build a few weapons, but most would find some degree of qualification to be desirable. Consider, for example, some analogous questions. How easy would it be for an inexperienced layman to perform an appendectomy? Or, how easy would it be for an untrained person to pilot a commercial airliner coast-to-coast in the U.S. (including the take-off and landing)? Neither of these tasks would be impossible, but would not the probabilities of success be increased if the "surgeon" were a biologist with some training in human anatomy and some experience with vivisection instead of a layman who had read a surgical textbook; or the "commercial pilot" held a license to fly private light aircraft rather than being self-taught through reading? In like manner, the probability of success of the terrorist bomb fabricators would be improved greatly if there were a team of about half a dozen technically trained and mechanically adept individuals involved in the project. Desirable fields of expertise include physics, chemistry, metallurgy, electronics, and the handling and use of high explosives. If the project were to proceed with complete disregard to reliability and safety, a fairly high probability of major accidents should be expected. Handling near-critical masses of fissile materials is a dangerous business, and the handling and storage of substantial quantities of high explosives can be equally risky.

The materials necessary to build a nuclear weapon include high explosives, Special Nuclear Material (SNM), and, depending upon the weapon design, some more or less sophisticated electronics. The SNM may be either ^{239}Pu, ^{235}U, or ^{233}U.

Acquiring the SNM is probably the major obstacle to be overcome if the terrorists are to construct a weapon. Natural uranium consists mainly of two isotopes, ^{235}U (about 0.7 percent), and ^{238}U (about 99.3 percent). The less abundant isotope is the readily fissionable species, and the uranium must be highly enriched in ^{235}U to be of practical use in a weapon. Two processes, gaseous diffusion and gas centrifuge, make use of the mass difference between the isotopes to selectively remove ^{238}U. A third process has been under development for several years, and the Department of Energy announced recently that a production plant using that process is planned to be operational by about 1991. The process involves selective ionization of ^{235}U with tuned lasers, and then electromagnetic separation of the charged ^{235}U from the neutral ^{238}U.

^{233}U does not occur naturally, and ^{239}Pu only occurs in insignificant amounts. Both of these isotopes must be made artificially in reactors. Plutonium is made by bombarding ^{238}U with neutrons to produce ^{239}U by neutron capture. Subsequently, two beta decays produce first ^{239}Np, which has a short half-life, and then the long-lived ^{239}Pu. Similarly, ^{233}U is made by neutron capture in the ^{232}Th to form ^{233}Th, which beta-decays through ^{233}Pa to ^{233}U.

Both gaseous diffusion and centrifuge enrichment facilities are very large, expensive, and difficult to fabricate. Such facilities are probably beyond the reach of terrorist groups, and theft is the most probable means by which they could obtain highly enriched ^{235}U.

^{239}Pu is the most widely available SNM. In addition to being produced for weapon use, it is made as a by-product within the fuel of power reactors. There are many kinds of reactors in operation, but the most common are the light-water reactors that employ low-enriched uranium as a fuel. The low-enriched uranium is not suitable for weapon use, but during the course of reactor operation some of the ^{238}U is converted to ^{239}Pu as described above. Another popular type of reactor is the Canadian heavy-water reactor, known as the CANDU, which uses natural uranium as a fuel and also produces plutonium. In addition, breeder reactors use plutonium as a fuel, and they are designed to produce more plutonium than is used during operations. A few reactors that use highly-enriched uranium as fuel and which breed ^{233}U from ^{232}Th have been produced, but ^{233}U is probably not sufficiently available to be considered viable for weapons use.

Fortunately, the plutonium that is made in power reactors is trapped in the highly radioactive residues of the fuel from which it is made. Plutonium represents only about one-half of one percent of the spent fuel from a light-water power reactor. In addition to unused uranium and plutonium, the residues of the fuel contain many radioactive fission products and various other radioisotopes that result from neutron-capture reactions, including some undesirable isotopes of plutonium. More than a ton of this spent fuel must be processed to obtain enough plutonium for one weapon.

Reprocessing spent reactor fuel to obtain plutonium requires large, expensive facilities with extensive radiation shielding. Even a small scale reprocessing plant suitable to obtain plutonium for a few weapons represents a substantial establishment. Moreover, the physical construction of the fuel assemblies negates the possibility of thefts of small quantities of spent fuel from the reactor storage area. Shielding and cooling during transport present additional problems of substantial magnitude when large quantities of spent fuel are involved.

All things considered, it appears that theft of already reprocessed plutonium is the most likely route for the terrorists to obtain the fuel. This fact limits the present availability of plutonium considerably. The five nuclear powers (the United States, the Soviet Union, China, the United Kingdom, and France) have plutonium processing plants as parts of their weapons programs, but the only commercial reprocessing plant for spent power-reactor fuel that is operational is in La Hague, France. The United Kingdom, West Germany, Japan, and the Soviet Union plan commercial reprocessing operations in the near future. Also, the option to reprocess fuel to extract the plutonium is still open to the United States, since all spent fuel is still in temporary storage at reactor sites in this country. Thus, the quantity of plutonium available from reprocessed reactor fuel is expected to show a marked increase in the near future. Presumably, this plutonium will be more susceptible to theft than the weapon plutonium, but use of plutonium extracted from spent fuel presents some problems.

Once ^{239}Pu is formed by the method described above, it remains in an intense neutron radiation environment until the fuel is removed or the reactor is shut down. While in that environment, some of the plutonium atoms capture neutrons and become ^{240}Pu. Subsequently, neutron captures can also produce ^{241}Pu and ^{242}Pu. Plutonium that is made for weapons is removed from the reactor before large quantities of these heavier isotopes can be formed. Weapon plutonium typically contains six to eight percent ^{240}Pu and only trace amounts of ^{241}Pu and ^{242}Pu. When the reactor is run to optimize fuel usage for power production, the heavier isotopes, together with some ^{238}Pu that is also produced, account for 30 to 35 percent of the plutonium in the spent fuel. ^{240}Pu and ^{242}Pu fission spontaneously, producing a continuous neutron background. ^{241}Pu and daughter products are gamma emitters. The combined gamma and neutron radiation from the spent fuel plutonium produce a significant health hazard to people who work with the plutonium, even after it is separated from the other highly radioactive components of the spent fuel waste. The neutron background also presents a pre-initiation problem that can significantly complicate the design and production of weapons.

For a nuclear explosion to take place, the weapon must contain a sufficient amount of SNM to exceed a critical mass. The critical mass depends, among other things, on the shape of the material, its composition and density, and the presence of impurities that can remove neutrons. The mass of material required for criticality can be reduced by surrounding the SNM with a neutron reflector. If a neutron initiates a fission in a quantity of SNM that equals or exceeds a critical mass, a chain reaction commences and the material is likely to melt or possibly explode. Since stray neutrons are always present in the environment, it is necessary that, before detonation, a nuclear weapon should contain no piece of SNM that is as large as a critical mass.

Two general methods have been described for producing nuclear explosions. In the first method, two or more pieces of SNM, each less than a critical mass, are brought together to form one piece that exceeds a critical mass (i.e., they form a supercritical mass). This may be achieved in a gun-barrel device, in which an explosive propels one piece of SNM into another piece to form a supercritical assembly. This type of gun-assembly device was the type that was employed over Hiroshima.

The second method makes use of the fact that when a subcritical piece of SNM is compressed, its density may be increased sufficiently to make it supercritical. The compression may be achieved by means of a spherical arrangement of specially shaped charges (lenses) of High Explosives (HE). A subcritical sphere of SNM is placed in a cavity in the center of the HE. When the HE is set off by a system of detonators, an inwardly-directed spherical implosion wave is produced. When the implosion wave reaches the SNM, it compresses the latter to supercriticality. This type of weapon was employed over Nagasaki.

In both types, a suitable neutron source should introduce a neutron near the time of maximum supercriticality to initiate an explosive chain reaction.

Once a chain reaction commences, it proceeds very rapidly. If, during the assembly process, a chain reaction is initiated at or just after a state of criticality has been attained, the SNM will return to a subcritical state before it ever reaches a significant degree of supercriticality, and a full-scale nuclear explosion will not occur. This lowering of the degree of criticality is brought about by two processes. First, the fissions consume a portion of the SNM, and if a sufficient amount is consumed, the remainder could not be critical in any geometry. Second, the energy released during the fissioning will melt and distort the SNM or will result in a very low yield nuclear explosion, possibly a much smaller yield than the yield of the HE used in the device. The chain reaction will stop immediately once the SNM is no longer critical, although a few delayed fissions will occur. Slow assembly times and high neutron backgrounds both increase the probability of the pre-initiation described above. The time to proceed from being barely critical to supercriticality is much longer for a gun-assembly weapon than is the corresponding time for an implosion weapon. For this reason, even weapon-grade plutonium, with its much higher neutron background than uranium, is not considered to be a suitable fuel for a gun-assembly weapon. A gun-assembly weapon made with reactor-grade plutonium, with its even higher neutron background, would have little chance of success.

India is the only country to have detonated a device that was admittedly produced from reactor-grade plutonium. For the reasons discussed above, if the terrorist group were to use such plutonium as their SNM, they likely will be constrained to an implosion-type weapon. Such a weapon requires a high degree of sophistication in the design and fabrication of the electronics and the high explosives. Satisfactory functioning requires a nearly perfect spherical compression wave. Otherwise, the SNM will be deformed without reaching the density required for supercriticality. On the other hand, a properly designed implosion weapon, with perhaps a conservative over-design of the high explosives, could suffer pre-initiation and still produce a substantial "fizzle" yield that would be adequate for the terrorists' purposes.

The cost and technical problems associated with uranium separation, together with difficulties associated with obtaining weapons-grade plutonium and the design problems associated with the use of reactor-grade plutonium in weapons, undoubtedly have all contributed not only to deterring terrorists but also to a much slower rate of proliferation among countries than was generally forecast twenty years ago. The same difficulties may make theft of a weapon seem more attractive to terrorists today than acquiring the materials and constructing a weapon themselves.

Theft of a weapon would be a formidable undertaking, but so would be theft of weapons-grade SNM. Theft of reactor-grade plutonium might be easier to accomplish, but that would entail the additional difficulties of handling, design, and construction discussed above. The United States' weapon systems are equipped with tamper-proof protective devices that are designed to prevent unauthorized use even by legitimate custodians. Successful employment of these systems by terrorists must be considered an extremely remote possibility. On the other hand, if a weapon were obtained from a country other than the United States, the possibility of successful use is probably not so remote. Even if the weapons are equipped with protective devices, the degree of sophistication of the devices is probably not equal to that of the United States. All in all, however, the probability of terrorists employing a nuclear weapon does not seem any greater today, nor will it be greater in the immediate future, than it has been during the last two decades.

The situation may change in the not-too-far distant future, however. The probability of terrorists acquiring and using a nuclear weapon may increase for two prime reasons.

First, there is a strong likelihood of proliferation of nuclear weapons possession beyond the five long-time nuclear powers and India in the reasonably near future, if it has not already occurred. It is widely believed that Israel and

South Africa may have nuclear weapons already, and, if they do not, that they could build weapons at any time that they desire to do so. Pakistan has had an operational gas centrifuge uranium enrichment plant for over a year. Only a small step is required to go from production of weapon-grade uranium to construction of a gun-assembly weapon. The government of Pakistan claims to have no interest in nuclear weapons, but it is hard to explain any other reason for having the separation plant. Both Brazil and Argentina are heavily involved in peaceful nuclear commerce, and both countries show indications that they intend to at least retain the option of weapon development. Such proliferation would make available to terrorists many more sources of materials and/or weapons, which could be obtained either by theft or by collusion with a disgruntled and rebellious member of a government.

Second, the construction of an operational laser isotope separation plant will undoubtedly be followed by articles in journals and the popular press, wherein all details of the processes will become public knowledge. When this occurs, it will be feasible for the first time for organized terrorist groups to consider performing their own uranium enrichment. Such a plant will not require as great a capital investment as either gaseous diffusion or gas centrifuge, and it will consume only a small fraction of the energy used by a gaseous diffusion plant. Natural uranium is inexpensive and fairly readily available for use in the enrichment process. Possession of enriched uranium could be followed in short order by construction of a gun-assembly nuclear weapon. Handling and working with uranium is much simpler than with plutonium, and the design and construction of a perhaps crude gun-assembly weapon requires minimal expertise compared to a spherical implosion weapon.

A prime threat would seem to come from some of the smaller countries with relatively undeveloped technological and industrial capabilities. Terrorist activities may appear attractive to the leaders of some of these countries who desire to exert influence beyond their own borders but who lack the military or industrial power to do so. In some cases governments have openly supported terrorist activities, while in other cases strong suspicions of such support exist in spite of denials by the governments concerned. Undoubtedly, some such governments harbor desires for nuclear weapons. They would welcome nuclear proliferation to countries with whom they could deal, or the development of a technology that they could install in their country either openly or subversively. Opportunity for either one or both of these methods for such governments to acquire nuclear weapons appears likely to be available in the future.

In summary, it is technically feasible for a terrorist organization to pose a nuclear threat at any time, but the probability of such a threat does not appear to be very high at present or for the immediate future. The probability of such a threat should increase dramatically, however, with the expected proliferation of nuclear weapon technology, and especially with the availability of an economical method of uranium enrichment.

What do you consider to be the important uncertainties in the TTAPS (Turco et al., 1983) calculations that a nuclear war would lead to "nuclear winter"? *(Respondent: Robert Ehrlich)*

The postulated drop in temperature following a nuclear war arises due to the blockage of sunlight caused by smoke and dust thrown up into the atmosphere. The smoke arises from fires caused by the nuclear detonations (primarily urban fires), while the dust arises due to the presence of numerous ground burst weapons. The numerous uncertainties in the TTAPS calculation in part relate to the values they assume for the amount of smoke and dust produced and the heights to which they are injected. Such questions as:

- What fraction of all cities will be attacked?
- What fraction of cities will burn?
- What is the average fuel density in cities?
- How often will firestorms occur?
- How high will smoke from firestorms be injected?
- Will fires be put out by blast?
- How long will fires continue to burn?

are all crucial in determining the amount of smoke. Similar questions arise concerning dust. Unfortunately, numerical estimates for each of these above quantities are just that, i.e., estimates that are very crudely projected. The end result for the temperature drop depends critically on all these parameters and it can vary widely as any one of them is changed. When all parameters are allowed to vary within their known limits, the variation in the output temperature drop is enormous.

In addition to the very large uncertainties in each of the TTAPS model's "input parameters," there are at least three other important types of uncertainties:

Model Defects

TTAPS uses a very primitive one-dimensional model in which all the smoke and dust is artificially assumed to arise instantaneously from every point on the earth's surface. Other calculations have been attempted using more correct three dimensional models, and these give average temperature declines between one-third and two-thirds those of TTAPS. However, even these calculations are still at a very primitive stage. (These are the same models used to predict weather.)

Scavenging

The rate of rainout of soot and dust depends on the degree of turbulence in the atmosphere. In the TTAPS calculation a kind of temperature inversion results in which there is very little chance for smoke and dust to be removed by rainout. In the actual atmosphere, it seems likely that the patchiness of smoke would cause large thermal gradients and much turbulence leading to a rapid rainout. This effect could lead to a totally negligible temperature decline.

Scenarios

The large temperature decline in the TTAPS calculation results primarily from smoke rather than dust, since the black soot particles tend to block light more than dust particles. However, if a nuclear attack is primarily directed against missile silos (counterforce attack) rather than cities, the particulate matter thrown up would be mainly dust rather than smoke, and the temperature decline would be significantly less.

Taking all the above uncertainties together, a fair assessment would be that following a large-scale nuclear war, a temperature decline could be anything between a totally negligible value and a very severe value -- an assessment, incidently, with which the TTAPS authors would not disagree.

If one gave the TTAPS authors the benefit of the doubt about a large temperature decline resulting from a large-scale nuclear war, do you believe in the validity of their assertion that such a large decline could result from a small nuclear war as well, that is, the 100-megaton "threshold"? *(Respondent: Robert Ehrlich)*

The idea that even a small nuclear war could give rise to nuclear winter is highly dependent on a rather artificial assumption concerning weapons targeting. In order for 100 megatons (less than one percent of the strategic arsenals), to give rise to a large temperature drop, one must assume that 1,000 weapons of 0.1 megaton yield are each delivered against different urban areas causing them all to burn. The TTAPS authors (Turco et al., 1983) recognize this to be a highly artificial scenario, and they include it in their paper not as a realistic prediction, but merely to make the point that even 100 megatons can cause a large temperature drop under certain extreme conditions. However, at least one of the TTAPS authors (Carl Sagan) has often neglected to remind his audience that this 100-megaton threshold is only a threshold under the most artificial kind of scenario. Even taking the TTAPS results at face value, the 5,000-megaton counterforce nuclear war would result in only one-quarter the temperature drop as the 100 megaton "threshold" -- 50 times the megatonnage, yet only one quarter the temperature drop! Sagan has called for a reduction in the arsenals to below 100 megatons so as to avoid nuclear winter. It seems likely that Sagan's belief that a 99 percent reduction in the arsenals is desirable is much more motivated by a political assessment than a scientific finding that there, in fact, exists a 100-megaton threshold.

If further research should somehow validate the important assumptions of the TTAPS calculations, do you believe that would mean "Taps" for Civil Defense? *(Respondent: Robert Ehrlich)*

First, I do not believe the "nuclear winter" issue will ever be definitively settled. The uncertainties are so large that the relevant parameters will never be pinned down with enough precision. However, let us suppose that government leaders come to *believe* that there is a good chance a large temperature drop could occur. In that case, it is quite possible that they could take actions which would reduce the likelihood of a catastrophic temperature decline even if nuclear war should occur. The most important factor would be the avoidance of targeting cities.

It is important to realize that "nuclear winter" is not a specific prediction. Everything really depends on how large the temperature decline would be. As far as Civil Defense is concerned, one can imagine temperature declines so drastic that virtually all plant and animal life in the northern hemisphere would be killed. Ecologists who work with the TTAPS results to forecast their ecological implications often use these "worst case" results, even though the TTAPS authors themselves note that such catastrophic temperature declines (60°C or 108°F) are extremely unlikely.

If the temperature declines really were that huge, Civil Defense probably would be futile. In the case of more moderate (*and much more likely*) temperature declines, Civil Defense would not be futile at all, but could very well be essential to survival. If a temperature decline should dramatically reduce agricultural yields, the Civil Defense measure of storing a year's supply of food, for example, assumes great importance. Civil Defense is, therefore, similar to government insurance (e.g., F.D.I.C.) on bank deposits. One can imagine financial crises so great that the government insurance is unable to protect depositors; however, for lesser disasters, the insurance *can* protect depositors. It seems silly to argue against the F.D.I.C. just because it cannot protect against the worst possible financial catastrophe.

It is understood that the electromagnetic pulse (EMP) produced by nuclear detonations can cause severe damage to unprotected electrical equipment. Would you expect that the EMP produced in a major nuclear attack on this country would in effect knock out the power distribution and telephone systems? (*Respondent: Russell P. Gates, II*)

EMP is characterized as a electromagnetic wave with high intensity fields of short duration. Experiments indicate that EMP can cause damage and/or malfunctions in power distribution and telephone systems. This damage can occur practically instantaneously over very large areas, possibly crippling vital systems. To assure there would be a continuing communications capability with the public in the event of a nuclear attack, the federal government is sponsoring a program to provide EMP protection and emergency power supplies to selected broadcast stations. To date, some 125 stations have been provided such protection.

Would you expect the EMP to damage critical components in laboratory and portable radiation measuring equipment so as to make them inoperable? (*Respondent: Russell P. Gates, II*)

This would depend on the sensitivity of the critical components that comprise the structure of the equipment. Normally, these devices are designed in such a manner as to protect them from EMP.

What would be the EMP effects on the newer automobiles that rely on solid state electronic ignition systems, and in other equipment, such as computers, that utilize advanced technology electronics? (*Respondent: Russell P. Gates, II*)

This is of concern to everyone studying EMP protection. The present use of non-metallic materials in the construction of vehicles only increases the vulnerability of the high technology electronics now being utilized in the new automobiles.

Are there practical ways to protect against EMP damage either by pre-manufacture design changes or by improvisation? For example, would the metal shielding provided in the trunk of an automobile protect devices that have been placed therein? (*Respondent: Russell P. Gates, II*)

Yes, the most practical way to protect against EMP is in the preliminary design phase before manufacture. However, retrofitting can also provide protection, but is not deemed the ultimate protection, and it is not very cost effective in most instances. Metal shielding of an automobile trunk will provide some protection for items placed therein. This probably would be the safest place in an automobile to store such items.

What are the differences in U.S. and Soviet views on Civil Defense? (*Respondent: Leon Gouré*)

Both the United States' and the Soviet Union's Civil Defense programs are of long standing, and the objectives of both are to save lives and mitigate the consequences of peace-time and war-caused disasters, including those which may result from nuclear strikes. Yet, from the standpoints of actual capabilities, scope and comprehensiveness, as well as funding, the two programs are very different, especially in the area of protection against and dealing with the consequences of a nuclear attack.

In the case of the United States, the relative absence of Civil Defense capability to deal with a possible nuclear war results from a number of factors. The latter can be grouped into three categories: views on the effectiveness of Civil Defense; views on the possible implications of Civil Defense for strategic stability; and cost considerations.

The first category includes two basic views. One of these derives from the widely believed popular worst-case scenarios which assume a massive Soviet surprise "out-of-the-blue" attack on all significant U.S. urban areas or triggered by a U.S. attempt to evacuate the population from high-risk areas. Such scenarios predict catastrophic population losses, especially in the absence of blast shelters, as well as a post-attack environment, which would result in further major losses among survivors from radioactive fallout, starvation, and disease. Another view is that although Civil Defense measures may significantly reduce human losses, they cannot prevent them altogether, and consequently, the probable loss of ten, twenty, or more percent of the population is "unacceptable" and vitiates the utility of Civil Defense, even though it could enhance prospects for survival of many others.

The second category derives from the "Mutually Assured Destruction" (MAD) concept as a desirable, or at least for the present, necessary form of mutual deterrence and strategic stability. This concept assumes that to ensure strategic stability and mutual deterrence, both the United States and the Soviet Union will continue not only to rely on their offensive strategic deterrent but also to leave their populations deliberately in hostage to each other. Consequently, any attempt by the United States to protect its population is seen as "destabilizing." There is also another view which holds that if the American people could be protected, and the consequences of a nuclear war could be mitigated by Civil Defense measures, the United States leadership may act more aggressively and possibly provoke a general nuclear war.

The third category of factors which have caused the United States to fail to develop an effective Civil Defense system is its possible cost. The cost factor has led to opposition to a Civil Defense program both from within and outside the government. Of course, the cost depends on the character of the program chosen and its rate of implementation. Any Civil Defense program which seeks to attain significant capabilities to protect the population will take years to implement. It is estimated that the development of plans and capabilities to carry out the rapid relocation of the population from high-risk areas in the event of a war threat will cost some $3.5 billion over a period of five to seven years, and that a program to provide all residents in such areas with protection in blast shelters may cost some $60 billion over a period of ten to twenty more years. To date, Congress has not been willing to commit itself to fund such programs.

One additional factor is that according to the Federal Civil Defense Act of 1950, which is still in force, U.S. Civil Defense is based on a "voluntary" partnership of federal, state, and local governments. Therefore, each state and locality is free to decide to what extent, if at all, it is willing to participate in Civil Defense planning and measures against a nuclear war threat. Of course, the participation of various critical private institutions and professional organizations, for example, hospitals, associations of engineers, physicians, nurses, etc., is also entirely voluntary.

In the Soviet Union, Civil Defense is based on different premises, as well as different political, administrative, and economic systems. The basic Soviet assumption is that because of the "inevitable" struggle between the East and West, war between them is a realistic possibility and, consequently, the Soviet Union must be prepared not only to deter aggression but also fight a nuclear war. No war-fighting doctrine or strategy can be meaningful without the objective of the Soviet Union's war survival. Thus, the Soviets point out that in the nuclear age, "the fate of states will be decided not only on the battlefield but also in the depth of their territory," and, consequently, that "protection of the homeland against enemy attack has become one of the most important tasks during a war." The Soviets, therefore, view Civil Defense as an integral part of their defense capability and strategy, and they consistently reject the U.S. concept of strategic stability based on a balance of mutual assured destruction.

While recognizing the limitations of Civil Defense, the Soviets do not believe that they will fail to have warning of an enemy attack, although they are attempting to develop a state of Civil Defense readiness which would be effective even under conditions of relatively short warning time. By and large, however, the Soviets believe it is likely that if a war were to occur, it would escalate slowly and give them sufficient time to implement all planned Civil Defense measures, including the relocation of the population from threatened civilian areas. Of course, Soviet Civil Defense planners do not expect Civil Defense to prevent massive damage to the economy or substantial losses among the population, although some Soviet manuals claim that these losses would not exceed those suffered by the Soviet Union in World War II. In the Soviet view, however, significant losses in no way invalidate the utility of Civil Defense, which they expect to be able to insure the survival not only of a majority of the population but also, more importantly, of its most valuable element, i.e., the leadership element at all levels: the elite, essential industrial and scientific workers, and so forth. In short, the Soviets believe that Civil Defense can make a critical contribution to the twin objectives of the survival of the communist system and of the Soviet Union as a nation and power.

In the Soviet Union, therefore, Civil Defense is a national program under military control, compulsory for all segments of government, the economy, and the general population. The participation of the citizenry in Civil Defense is considered to be mandated by the Soviet Constitution, which requires all citizens to contribute to the strengthening of Soviet might and to the country's defense. Officially, it is said that the Communist Party leadership and the Soviet government pay unremitting attention to the further strengthening and perfecting of the U.S.S.R. Civil Defense.

Being a part of the Soviet defense capabilities, the Soviets apparently do not balk at the cost of a comprehensive Civil Defense program, despite a GNP which is only one-half to two-thirds of that of the United States.

What is the nature of the Soviet Civil Defense Program? *(Respondent: Leon Gouré)*

In contrast with the United States, which has yet to develop and implement an effective long-range national Civil Defense program for a possible nuclear war situation, the Soviet Union has a long standing, comprehensive, well organized and well financed national Civil Defense program which encompasses all segments of government, the economy, and the population. The Soviet program can be said to be realistic, because it combines a correct appreciation of the threat and of the effects of nuclear weapons with the development of necessary organization, plans, forces, capabilities and means which can significantly mitigate the consequences of enemy nuclear strikes for the population and the economy under conditions of various attack scenarios.

Underlying the Soviet Civil Defense program are a number of important assumptions. First, it is not expected to bear alone the full brunt of an enemy nuclear attack. Instead, Civil Defense is only one element of a Soviet war survival capability and strategy which combines offensive preemptive Soviet counterforce strikes and large-scale active defense (anti-ballistic missiles, anti-air, and anti-satellite defenses) intended to weaken the enemy attack, with passive (i.e., Civil Defense) measures which will deal with the consequences of the strikes by the residual enemy nuclear weapons which will reach their targets. Second, the Soviet Union does not expect an enemy surprise attack "out of the blue." It allows for both short and protracted warning of an attack. However, most of the present Soviet Civil Defense system appears to be based on the expectation, indeed the requirement, that an attack would be preceded by days or weeks of warning. Third, Soviet Civil Defense does not anticipate that the United States would target the Soviet population or cities and the general economy *per se*. While the Soviets believe that some cities, because of their special importance as administrative, transportation and defense-industry centers, may be attacked and that others may suffer collateral damage from strikes on nearby military installations, the Soviets do not share a popular American view that in a nuclear war, all substantial cities should be expected to be struck.

The primary mission of Soviet Civil Defense is threefold. First, it provides protection of the population from nuclear, chemical, and bacteriological weapons effects and the sustaining of the survivors in the post-attack environment, with priority given to leadership elements at all levels, the elite, essential industrial workers, and the Civil Defense forces. This is accomplished through a program of blast shelter construction in high-risk locations, detailed planning and preparations for the rapid relocation and dispersal of residents from risk areas to rural areas, and the protection of personnel in non high-risk areas in fallout shelters. Second, it protects the economy, including utilities, industry, transportation, and agricultural resources, and creates necessary stocks of food, fuel, supplies, and equipment to sustain survivors, and aids in the rapid reconstitution of essential industrial and agricultural production. This includes a variety of measures, including hardening, dispersal, duplication, rapid shut-down and evacuation. Third, it is responsible for the implementation of large-scale post-strike rescue, damage-limiting, repair and restoration operations by the mass of civilian and military Civil Defense forces, medical assistance to and treatment of the injured, and the restoration of damaged utilities, industrial enterprises, transportation, bridges, and so on, as well as decontamination of surviving equipment, supplies, buildings, roads and, where necessary, ground surfaces.

In order to be able to deal with the magnitude of the potential damage and casualties and to implement the great scope of necessary Civil Defense measures, the Soviets believe in the requirement of preparing large, trained and equipped Civil Defense forces (estimated at some sixteen to twenty million people), backed by military Civil Defense units. They also believe in instructing the entire population, from school children to retirees, in Civil Defense, on a compulsory basis. The recruitment of Civil Defense forces is facilitated by the inclusion, largely on a compulsory basis, of a high percentage of industrial workers, all municipal, transportation, and construction workers including fire and police, the entire medical and public health system and personnel, a major part of the agricultural work force, employees of the service and trade sector, and so on.

The seriousness with which the Soviet leadership views the utility of their Civil Defense is reflected in the level of investments in it, which constitutes a rather significant burden for the Soviet economy. According to current U.S. intelligence estimates, only four elements of the program dealing with personnel and shelter construction are believed to represent a U.S. equivalent cost of some $3 billion per year. The total cost of the program in U.S. equivalent costs has been variously estimated at some $5 to $6 billion per year, compared with the current U.S. federal budget for Civil Defense of $140 million per year.

The Soviet leadership has good reasons to believe that its Civil Defense program will be able, in the event of a nuclear war, to markedly reduce Soviet losses and enhance the prospects of the Soviet Union's national survival as well as that of the Soviet system. This is confirmed by many U.S. studies of the consequences of U.S. retaliatory strategic strikes on the Soviet Union in scenarios where it is assumed that it has been able to implement its Civil Defense measures, especially the relocation of the population from high-risk areas. It should be noted that at the present time, pre-attack relocation of the population and of Civil Defense forces from high-risk areas remains the Soviet method for their protection and for ensuring the capability of Civil Defense forces to carry out this post-strike mission.

What are the probable Soviet perceptions of a stepped-up U.S. Civil Defense effort? *(Respondent: Leon Gouré)*

In assessing Soviet views on any U.S. defense policy, it is essential to distinguish between real Soviet perceptions and Soviet propaganda. All too often, the latter is mistakenly considered by many people in the West as reflecting actual Soviet views or fears, especially when the propaganda, as it is intended to do, serves to reinforce the views, concerns, and biases of such people on defense issues.

Officially, the Soviet Union is critical of any and all U.S. defense efforts and changes in what it claims to be the existing U.S.-Soviet military balance. Soviet spokesmen like to assert that given what they allege to be the "aggressive nature of imperialism," i.e., the West, "strength in the hands of imperialism is a source of military danger, while in the hands of socialism [i.e., the U.S.S.R. and its allies], it is a source for insuring peace and lessening the threat of war." It follows from this that Soviet propaganda periodically claims that the U.S. Civil Defense program, whose scope it tends to exaggerate, reflects U.S. preparations for war and continued fighting because it seeks to create the "illusion" that the United States could survive a nuclear war. At the same time, Soviet propaganda and propagandists, when addressing Western audiences, seek to either deny the existence of a Soviet Civil Defense program or to play down its significance.

In reality, the Soviets regard Civil Defense as a rational and essential element of a country's defense posture in the nuclear age because no country can reasonably be expected to leave itself totally vulnerable to a possible enemy attack. The Soviets have dismissed the Western argument that the Soviet Civil Defense program has any effect on the U.S.-Soviet strategic balance, claiming instead, as Brezhnev did in 1976, that the program's objective is solely humanitarian, because the Soviet government has a duty to protect the Soviet people. For this reason, the Soviets have refused to include the question of Civil Defense in any of the SALT negotiations despite U.S. urging to do so. Instead, they claim that because of the Soviet Union's "peace policy," Soviet Civil Defense "does not incite, does not promote, and does not provide impetus to war," but, on the contrary, that it "intensifies that peaceful actions taken by our state [i.e., the Soviet Union] and strengthens international security as a whole."

There is no reason why the objectives of U.S. Civil Defense would be any less humanitarian than those of the Soviet program. While the Soviets would prefer the United States to remain totally vulnerable to Soviet nuclear strikes, there are several reasons why increased U.S. Civil Defense efforts would not be perceived by the Soviets as an indication of increased U.S. belligerency. First, the development of effective Civil Defense capabilities takes a long time, indeed many years. Despite some thirty years of efforts and large investments, the Soviet Union is still far from having achieved all of its Civil Defense objectives. Secondly, Soviet strategic doctrine does not target the U.S. population *per se*, and Soviet strategy would remain unaffected by possible reductions in U.S. population losses. Thirdly, the Soviets are well aware, as is evident from their own Civil Defense literature, that Civil Defense by itself does not negate the effectiveness of strategic deterrence or make aggression more likely because it cannot prevent massive damage to the economy and society or major losses among the population. Finally, as already noted, the Soviets view Civil Defense as a logical necessity given, the magnitude of potential destruction in a nuclear war and the natural desire of any state to mitigate its consequences.

In general, Soviet perceptions of the level of U.S. belligerency at any given time are not determined by any single defense program, but by a combination of factors, including not only U.S. strategic capabilities, but also political attitudes and especially U.S. sensitivities to a specific international issue or crisis in U.S.-Soviet relations. Soviet experience suggests that if U.S. strategic superiority in the 1960s and early 1970s did not actually make the U.S. dangerously belligerent *vis-a-vis* the Soviet Union, an increased U.S. Civil Defense effort in the 1980s in the face of Soviet strategic parity, if not superiority, is very much more unlikely to have such an effect on U.S. behavior.

How does one get an appreciation for the fallout radiation dose rates and doses that might occur over this country in the event of a nuclear attack? *(Respondent: Jack C. Greene)*

No one can predict with any degree of reliability the amount of radioactivity that would result from a nuclear attack or how this radioactivity would be distributed over the country. There are too many unknowns (indeed, unknowables). Among them are:

- The type of attack (population, industry, military, demonstration or various combinations);

- Weapon details (megatonnage [MT] per individual bomb, fission/fusion ratios, fusing provisions--i.e., to detonate on contact or at a specific altitude, accuracy, etc.);

- The weight and timing of an attack (total megatonnage delivered over what period of time and in what season);

- The weather (wind directions and speeds, snow, rain, temperature, etc., at the time of the attack); and

- Weather conditions following the attack (winds and rain would effect the movement of the fallout and the leaching of the radioactivity into the soil, etc.).

Thus, in characterizing some particular post-attack radiological environment, it is necessary to make a number of assumptions:

- Assume an enemy attempted to launch a 10,000 MT attack on the United States. (This is a very heavy attack, but probably within the capability of the Soviet Union now or in the future).

- Assume that two-thirds, or 6,670 MT, arrive on the 50 states of the U.S. (This allows for malfunctions and such things as abortive take-offs and the like).

- Assume that two-thirds of the megatons that arrive on the U.S. are ground burst. (This may be high. It may be low. There is no way of knowing).

- Assume that 50 percent of the explosive power of the weapons is due to fission and 50 percent is due to fusion. (The fission process contributes to the fallout radioactivity. The contribution from the fusion is relatively small and therefore is ignored).

- Assume that each ground burst fission-megaton produces a one hour dose rate of about two million roentgens per hour per square mile. (This is the so-called K factor, which has been determined from experience at the Nevada and the Pacific test sites. The two million figure refers to the dose rate that would be produced over a large smooth plane if the fallout were evenly distributed and if the measurement data were taken after the fallout deposition had ceased and were then normalized to one hour post-detonation. This may sound complicated, but what it really specifies is what part of the total radioactivity produced in the explosion comes down in the local fallout).

- Assume that about 20 percent of the radioactivity produced by the attack blows out to sea and therefore does not contribute to the dose over the U.S. land area.

- Assume the land area of the 50 states of the U.S. totals about 3.6 million square miles. (If you want to leave out Hawaii and Alaska, the number is about 3 million square miles).

- Assume that the presence of terrain features such as hills, gullies, trees and unevenness in the ground surface and buildings would on the average reduce the "smooth plane" exposure rates by a factor of about 2. (In some cases the reduction could be less, in others considerably more).

Now applying these assumptions, we can calculate the average (mean) standard exposure rate over the United States by multiplying these factors together as follows:

$(10^4)(.67)(.67)(.5)(2 \times 10^6)(.8)(1/3.6 \times 10^6)(.5) = 493$ R/hr, which we round off to 500 R/hr.

If we want to estimate dose for, say, the first four days, we multiply by factors (which are "effective times" related to how long the fallout remains aloft before hitting the ground) to convert this exposure rate to exposure. These factors range from about 1.5 to 3.0 "effective" hours depending on the calculated time of arrival. In this example, let us take an average of 2.25 and get 500 x 2.25 = 1,125 R. (The four-day dose is often used as a basis for estimating fallout radiation casualties.) If one wants to make different assumptions, of course one can do so.

Keep in mind that the numbers we have estimated are averages. In some places, downwind from a field of missile silos, for example, the exposure rates could be much higher. In other places they would be lower and in some places there would be no fallout at all. (Because the high altitude winds tend to blow from the west to the east, the average dose rates along the east coast would be about twice those toward the far west). Also keep in mind that a ten-thousand-megaton attack is a very large attack. Many scenarios result in postulated attacks that are much smaller and would produce proportionately smaller exposure rates.

Now suppose we want an idea of how these doses and dose rates would vary over the country. To achieve this we have to make another assumption, namely that we have a reasonably good fallout model (a way to simulate the distribution of the radioactive material that would be created by a nuclear explosion in accordance with some wind pattern that we specify. This means that we have a computer fallout model which, when we specify the type of burst, the weapon characteristics and the wind patterns, can produce a reasonable depiction of what the fallout pattern would be like).

Based on computer studies at the Institute For Defense Analysis, Table B shows how an average dose rate of 500 R/hr and an average 4-day dose of 1,125 R might vary over the country.

Table B. Calculated Distribution of Dose Rates and Doses Over the U.S.

% U.S. Land Area	Dose Rate Range (R/hr) From	To	Four-Day Dose (R) From	To
10	0	110	0	170
20	110	220	170	330
35	220	520	330	830
20	520	990	830	1700
14	990	1650	1700	3300
1	1650	3300	3300	10000

Notes for Table B:

The dose rates in the second and third columns are the so-called standard dose rates. These are the rates that would occur at one hour post detonation if all the fallout were deposited by that time.

The last two columns refer to the dose expected during the first four days following the assumed attack. As mentioned above, this four-day dose often is used as an index of the amount of acute biological damage expected from exposure to fallout radiation.

In the calculations that produced the above numbers, it was assumed that all the weapons were detonated at the same time.

How would the dose rates produced by the radioactive fallout resulting from a nuclear attack on this country be expected to change with time? *(Respondent: Jack C. Greene)*

Starting from the dose rate data reported in the previous answer, one can estimate how these numbers would change with time. Through the process of radioactive decay, the dose rates reduce very rapidly at first and then more slowly as time passes. For about the first six months, the so-called seven-ten rule applies. After all the fallout is down on the ground, for every seven-fold increase in time since the weapons were detonated, radiation levels decrease by a factor of ten. After about six months the reduction in dose rates with time is even faster than the seven-ten rule would predict. (The seven-ten rule applies only if the fallout remains undisturbed--that is no decontamination operations are performed and the weathering effects are negligible--and only if the fallout is from weapons that were detonated at nearly the same time). Table C summarizes the projections.

Table C. Percentage of U.S. Land Areas Subjected to Various Dose-Rate Ranges at Various Times After the Assumed Attack.

(roentgens/hr.)

Time (post attack)	10%	20%	35%	20%	14%	1%	
one hour	0	110*	220*	520	990	1650	3300
2 days	0	1.1	2.2	5.2	9.9	16.5	33
3 days	0	0.69	1.4	3.2	6.1	10	21

(milliroentgens/hr)

100 hours	0	440	880	2080	3960	6600	13200
6 months	0	4.4	8.8	21	40	66	132
2 years	0	0.11	0.22	0.52	0.99	1.7	3.3
5 years	0	0.022	0.044	0.104	0.20	0.33	0.66
25 years	0	0.0011	0.0022	0.0052	0.01	0.017	0.033

Notes for Table C:

*That is, 10% of the land area experiences exposure rates between 0 and 110 R/hr, 20% between 110 and 220 R/hr, etc.

At 100 hours there is a switch from roentgens/hr to milliroentgens/hr.

All of the above values are based on the assumption that the fallout remains wherever it is deposited which, of course, is a poor assumption particularly at the later times. The important point is that the amount of radioactivity necessary to produce the above exposure rates would still be in existence at the times indicated. Radioactivity cannot be destroyed. Some might migrate or physically be moved out of harm's way, but the remainder would have to be dealt with. Wind, rain, traffic, decontamination, and other factors would cause the fallout material to move around. It is useful to think of the radioactive fallout as being much like a fine beach sand and thus subject to the same kinds of movements.

Is PF (Protection Factor) simply the ratio of outside dose rate to the dose rate to be expected inside a sheltered location? *(Respondent: Jack C. Greene)*

No.

PF as used for U.S. Civil Defense planning is defined as follows:

The Protection Factor is the ratio of the dose rate to be expected in a completely unprotected location compared to the dose rate expected with the same radionuclide (fallout) concentration in a protected location.

PF is a dimensionless number, and for all practical purposes, is always greater than one. A *completely unprotected location* has a unique meaning. It refers to a location 3 feet (1 meter) over a hypothetical smooth plane with a uniform density of fission products that are exactly 1.12 hours old. Thus, a protection factor of one could not occur in the real world since an infinite smooth plane cannot occur in the real world.

Almost any outside location would provide some protection. Ground roughness and the presence of structures and trees or lakes and ponds would reduce the dose rates from the values that would occur if the fallout were on an infinite smooth plane. This reduction easily could be by a factor of two or more. If some outside location provided a PF of two and if there were a PF-100 shelter subjected to the same amount of fallout, the relative "inside" vs. "outside" dose rates would be 50, and of course, this "outside" dose rate would vary from one place to another.

Thus, PF is a concept that has application for planning (pre-attack) purposes. A shelter with a PF of 100 would provide twice as much protection as a shelter with a PF of 50 and four times as much as a shelter with a PF of 25, assuming they were subjected to the same fallout risk. Thus, the concept of PF provides a basis for evaluating relative shelter radiation-protective quality. (Incidentally, the PF as assessed for any given structure is evaluated in terms of unoccupied space. If occupied to capacity, this value might be increased by a factor of two or more.)

In an actual fallout environment (post-attack), the concept of PF has little utility. In fact, it can easily cause confusion. The radiation environment in one shelter space as compared to another, or as compared to some outside location, can only be evaluated in any realistic way through use of radiation measuring instruments. A shelter with a rated value of 100 might have considerable lower dose rates than one of, say, 50, if the latter were subjected to lower levels of fallout or even none at all. (See Martin O. Cohen's discussion of protection factors; and Spencer, Chilton, and Eisenhauer, 1980.)

To distinguish the protection a structure might be expected to provide against fallout radiation as contrasted to initial radiation, the Federal Emergency Management Agency is recommending the use of FPF Fallout Protection Factor, as contrasted to PF, although the latter will be most often found in the literature.

How does one evaluate the expected biological consequences of various radiation exposures that could occur following a nuclear attack? *(Respondent: Jack C. Greene)*

Previous questions and answers dealt with the radiation levels and doses that might be expected following an assumed attack. These projections were presented in terms of the roentgen (R) unit. The roentgen, however, is not a generally familiar unit (like pounds, miles, minutes, etc.) and most people have little appreciation for the biological consequences to be expected from various radiation exposures. A simple exposition of expected radiation exposure effects is presented in Table D, taken from Report #42 issued by the National Council on Radiation Protection and Measurements (NCRP, 1974).

Table D. Recommended System for Predicting Outcome of Gamma Radiation Exposure (the "Penalty" Table).

Medical care will be needed by	Accumulated radiation exposures (R) in any period of:		
	one week	one month	four months
NONE	150	200	300
SOME (5% may die)	250	350	500
MOST (50% may die)	450	600	-

Other forms of biological damage could occur even at exposure levels where there would be none of the acute effects such as nausea, vomiting, loss of hair or other signs of radiation sickness. Included would be higher-than-otherwise chances of developing cancer or leukemia and of producing offspring suffering from some type of genetic damage.

It is estimated that each roentgen of gamma radiation exposure increases the risk of developing some malignancy (cancer or leukemia) by about one or two chances in ten thousand.

In assessing genetic damage to the population, it is obvious that full account should be taken of the harm to be expressed in all future generations. An estimate of this risk would be about 30 to 40 such effects per million person roentgen, or, expressed differently, a risk of 30 to 40 per million per roentgen exposure. This is about one-third the value cited above for the risk of fatal radiation-induced cancer.

Perspective about the calculated post-attack dose rates can be drawn from an examination of peacetime levels of exposure and the safety limits that are applied in today's society.

The average dose in the United States from external terrestrial radionuclides is about 40 milliroentgens per year. This is about 0.0046 mR/hr. The average dose throughout the country from cosmic radiation is about 28 milliroentgens per year (0.0032 mR/hr). These doses, of course, vary from place to place. The highest whole-body total of 125 milliroentgen per year (0.014 mR/hr) from all sources represents the situation for the city of Denver, where both the cosmic and terrestrial components are higher than average.

The allowable maximum exposure for the general public (for other than medical purposes) recommended by the National Council on Radiation Protection and Measurements is 0.5 roentgens per year. If received at a constant rate over the year, this would be 0.057 mR/hr. The allowable maximum exposure for radiation workers (those working in nuclear power plants, uranium mines, nuclear medicine or radiology, etc.) is ten times that value, or 5 R/yr, which at a constant exposure rate would be 0.57 mR/hr.

For the assumptions that were used, we have reasonable confidence in the calculations about the various percentages of U.S. land areas being subjected to various amounts of fallout. Also, we have a reasonably good idea of the biological consequences of various radiation exposures. However, we have much less confidence in predicting which parts of the country might be affected and to what degree. At least theoretically, any section of the country is at risk in the event of a nuclear attack and could be subjected to serious levels of fallout. It is clear that the current peacetime exposure levels would be unachievable in many parts of the country for years to come. Even with an adequate number of quality radiological instruments, the radiation control problems would be immense--and without them, almost impossible to resolve.

If there were to be a nuclear attack on the United States, it seems likely that it would begin with the launching of missiles from Russian submarines lying off our coasts. Since the times of flight would be very short, the warning time at best would be only a few minutes. In this case, Civil Defense plans such as evacuating cities could not possibly work. Can you explain why such plans were ever promulgated in the first place? (Respondent: Jack C. Greene)

I can try. True, if a nuclear war were to start tomorrow, like a bolt out of the blue with a Pearl Harbor-type surprise attack by submarine-launched missiles aimed at our major coastal cities, there would be no time to get people out of the cities and all the effort spent in planning for city evacuation would have been futile. To the people most critical of the city evacuation planning program, this "out of the blue" scenario is probably the one they have in mind. And they could be right. It is possible that the Russians have already picked the date for this surprise attack, or decided on some set of circumstances when such an attack will be initiated.

I do not believe it.

If the Soviet leadership should decide to launch a surprise attack on the United States, they would have to do so without warning their own citizenry or evacuating their own cities, which we readily could detect. (City evacuation is a primary Soviet Civil Defense tactic which the Soviet Civil Defense literature claims would reduce casualties by some 100 million.) Also, there are many uncertainties about the success of the attack, and even if successful (whatever that means), there are tremendous uncertainties about the after effects, e.g., global fallout phenomena, the ozone problem, "nuclear winter," and so on.

I believe that the Russians are as wary of nuclear war as we are and that they believe as we do that no one could "win" such a war, if "win" is defined in any reasonable sense, such as being better off afterward than before.

Does this mean there will be no nuclear war? I think it probably does. But can we be sure? It is hard to feel secure when we know that some 40,000 nuclear warheads exist, many already aimed and ready to go, and when no nuclear arms limitation treaties exist. The achievement of programs to substantially reduce the world's nuclear arsenal to negligable amounts seems to be far in the future.

If we accept the proposition that both sides sincerely wish to avoid nuclear war, how could such a war occur?

Possibilities that have been suggested include:

- The "madman" scenario. A Hitler-type comes to power either in the Soviet Union or the United States or some other country with a substantial number of nuclear weapons, and because of his megalomaniacal delusions pushes the button.

- A malfunction in our (their) radar (computers) or other components of the surveillance equipment occurs, and we (they) think an attack has been launched and we (they) respond in kind.

- A third country (Libya, Iran) detonates a nuclear weapon in such a way as to make the U.S. (U.S.S.R.) think the other side did it and we (they) respond in kind.

- A U.S. (U.S.S.R.) General (Colonel) (Admiral) cannot stand the pressure and takes the matter into his own hands and launches an attack.

(This might be called the "Dr. Strangelove scenario.")

No doubt other possibilities exist. All of them sound pretty bizarre and far-fetched, but they could happen. The probability is small, probably very, very small, but nevertheless greater than zero. Who would have predicted that the assassination by a Serb of an obscure Austrian Archduke would bring about World War I?

There is another way a nuclear war could come about. "Things get out of hand." The Falkland Island experience is a prime example. Neither the British nor the Argentines wanted to get into a shooting war, but they did. Things just got out of hand. One side did something; the other countered; the confrontation escalated. And before they knew it, open warfare was underway. (Another term for this scenario is "miscalculation." One side underestimates [miscalculates] the impact on the other of some particular action, the other does the same, and the escalation continues.)

There seem to be many opportunities for "things to get out of hand" in our dealings with the Russians. The Persian Gulf, the Syria/Israel situation, Central America, and Poland are examples. Suppose that the Cuban missile crisis were to occur today. Would the Russians back down as they did in 1962 for President John Kennedy? Then, we clearly had nuclear superiority. Now we do not. With the nuclear parity that now exists, would such a confrontation escalate? Who knows?

I repeat, my feeling is that the odds against a nuclear war are very high because "everybody knows" such a war would be a catastrophe for all mankind. But as long as nuclear weapons exist and as long as we do not have a means to control their production, the possibility of nuclear war exists. And if such a war should occur, the "things get out of hand" scenario, I think, is much more likely than all of the other possibilities put together. Many people, of course, who have their own "pet" scenario would not agree.

In any event, there is a plausible case for city evacuation planning. In the "things get out of hand" scenario there would be a drawn-out period during which tension builds up. (For example, it was about two months after the Argentines occupied the Falklands before the British attacked.) At some stage the build-up of tension might become so severe that war would seem almost inevitable, and people, even without government direction or encouragement, would decide to get out of the probable target areas. Surely, realistic plans and preparations could help reduce the chaos that otherwise almost certainly would occur.

There is no doubt that the amount of fallout radioactivity to be expected in the event of a nuclear attack on this country would cause many additional casualties and in general make the process of recovery very difficult; but does not the threat of an enemy using "salted" weapons to enhance the amount of radioactivity make this threat much worse? *(Respondent: (by Jack C. Greene)*

Very probably not. There are two basic reasons. One is primarily technical, the other primarily tactical. Each is discussed in turn:

Technical

A way to increase the amount of fallout radioactivity produced by a nuclear explosion is to include in the bomb's design an element such as natural cobalt. (Natural cobalt contains 27 protons and 32 neutrons, and is called ^{59}Co.) When the bomb detonates some of this natural cobalt is changed to cobalt-60 (^{60}Co), a radioactive element emitting penetrating gamma rays. The mechanism is this: the non-radioactive natural cobalt captures a neutron that was produced in the explosion becoming ^{60}Co with 27 protons and 33 neutrons--an unstable element which therefore is radioactive. But for the early times after the bomb is detonated, up to months and even a few years, this ^{60}Co is far less radioactive than the other material produced in the explosion. Further, the neutron that was used to transform the natural cobalt into radioactive cobalt could as well have been used to irradiate natural uranium either to split it--producing energy and more neutrons and more "splits"--or to produce neptunium which also is radioactive--far more so than ^{60}Co. Any element other than cobalt that might be considered for "salting" has the same limitations. Thus from the technical point of view, the adding of some material such as cobalt to a bomb to increase the fallout radioactivity makes little sense.

Tactical

There is good reason to believe that the military tacticians on both sides have little interest in enhancing the radioactivity that could be produced by the weapons in their nuclear arsenals. Radioactive fallout, although a killer of people, has serious limitations as a military weapon. Its deposition cannot be accurately predicted being subject to local wind conditions and to many other uncertainties, and it readily can be protected against. (Fallout could not be counted on to immobilize a missile field or even an airfield.) However, perhaps the strongest reason why an attacker would not want to enhance the radioactivity output of his strategic weapons is that some of this radioactivity would go into the upper atmosphere to eventually be deposited on his own soil. This is a boomerang effect that is unavoidable.

In summary, the deliberate "salting" of a nuclear weapon makes little sense either technically or tactically.

Could farm animals be protected from radiation exposures in a nuclear attack? *(Respondent: Sumner A. Griffin)*

In the event of a full-scale nuclear attack, highly dangerous levels of fallout could cover large areas of the country, including much of the farmland and grazing areas. Without a practical means for protecting farm animals and reducing their radiation exposures, heavy losses would occur.

Most grazing livestock are located away from the target areas and would not be exposed to initial nuclear radiation. (This consists of the neutrons and gamma rays released almost instantaneously at the time of the burst.) Livestock could be exposed to the beta and gamma radiation from fallout downwind from surface bursts. Fallout radiation from air bursts or from worldwide fallout would have only minor effects on livestock.

While specialized structures for protection of livestock from fallout do not seem feasible under present conditions, the utilization of existing structures can provide significant differences in numbers of livestock that would be lost during a nuclear attack.

A cooperative study by the Oak Ridge National Laboratory and the Tennessee Office of the Statistical Reporting Service of the U.S. Department of Agriculture involving two surveys was done in Tennessee to determine what facilities and feed reserves were present on farms (Griffin, 1968; Griffin, 1969a; Griffin, 1969b; Griffin, Bressee and Shinn, 1969). In one survey the number of barns per farm was found to be 1.47 and in the other, 1.85. This indicated that 70 to 80 percent of all cattle could be sheltered indoors. Feed reserves ranging from 70 to 99 days were present, depending on the time of year. Radiation protection factors (PF's) were calculated according to the procedures and supporting data in the Rural Shelter Handbook (Texas A & M, undated). The average PF for the buildings reported in the survey was 1.8. This PF was a minimum value which did not consider ground roughness or the mutual shielding of animals by other animals in the barn. (If these additional factors had been taken into account the calculated PF's could have doubled or tripled.)

The value of a PF of 1.8 for cattle under an assumed hypothetical attack of about 3,500 megatons was determined. It was assumed that a gamma radiation exposure of about 550 roentgens over the first four-day period following a nuclear attack would kill about one-half of the cattle so exposed. Using this mid-lethal value of 550 roentgens, it was estimated that 33 percent of the Tennessee cattle would have died by the end of thirty days. When the PF was assumed to be unity (no protection), 60 percent of the animals were calculated to have received lethal exposures.

If farmers have adequate lead time before the arrival of fallout, livestock should be placed in whatever shelter is available. In this situation lactating dairy animals should have first priority for shelter and for feeds that had not been contaminated by fallout. This would minimize intake of radioisotopes of iodine that are readily accumulated in the milk (Bell and Blake, 1976).

In summary, in the event of a nuclear attack, efforts to protect farm animals could have a high pay off. Due to the rapid decay of early fallout radioactivity, even a few days of minimum protection could make a significant difference between their death and survival.

Would the meat from animals exposed to ionizing radiation resulting from a nuclear attack be safe for human consumption? *(Respondent: Sumner A. Griffin)*

In assessing the utility of meat for human consumption from animals exposed to radiation it is useful to look at two different situations:

The animals receive little or no exposure and signs of radiation sickness do not occur. In this case, the only questions about use of the meat would be those that apply in any other situation such as: Are the animals healthy? Is there adequate refrigeration to preserve the meat?

The animals have been exposed to heavy doses of fallout radiation, they show signs of radiation sickness, and their survivability may be in doubt.

Research with laboratory animals exposed to gamma, neutron, gamma plus neutron or x radiation indicates that animals exposed to lethal doses of whole body radiation may develop bacteremia (bacterial invasion of the circulatory system). If this occurred in meat animals it could severely limit their use for human consumption. However, in research at Oak Ridge with pigs and beef cattle, bacteremia did not occur as it had in the laboratory animals (Griffin and Eisele, 1971; Eisele and Griffin, 1969; Eisele and Griffin, 1970; Eisele and Bell, 1973).

In the Oak Ridge studies, pigs that had been exposed to gamma radiation and that showed symptoms of radiation sickness were slaughtered. Samples of blood, liver, lymph, heart and muscle did not show bacterial invasions. The cattle that were irradiated showed some slight bacterial presence. However, this occurred in both the controls and the cattle showing radiation sickness. Bacteremia was not indicated.

Use of the meat from animals that had died from radiation exposures is not recommended. This is because: (1) the animals would not have been bled; (2) there would be uncertainty about how long they had been dead; and (3) it is well known that bacterial activity expands very rapidly in a dead animal.

Animals showing radiation sickness should be slaughtered using ordinary procedures. However, caution should be used to prevent contamination from external sources and from the intestinal tract. Animals are excellent screeners of radiative fallout--there is limited absorption through the walls of the stomach and the intestines and a rapid excretion of the fission products. Thus the body organs would be the locations of highest activity. Organ meats, (e.g., liver, heart) should not be used.

Animals should be slaughtered as needed unless adequate refrigeration and transportation for distribution is available. In preparing the meat from animals exposed to radiation, the preferred method of cooking would be in water, and the water should be discarded afterward. If animals had been on pasture and had ingested contaminated feeds, it would be preferable to remove the bones before cooking.

In view of the evidence available, the use of meat from animals exposed to radiation and showing signs of radiation sickness could be used for human consumption. Animals are good filters for fission products and bacteremia does not appear to be a problem in meat animals. The problems that would occur in a nuclear attack and the other hazards that would be present would be far greater than any problems from using meat from animals showing radiation sickness. (For further information, see Silverman et al., 1957; Kossakowski, 1968; Wasserman and Trum, 1955; and Pawel, Kalousova and Vranovska, 1967.)

Why is the Civil Defense Agency involved in the development and production of radiological instruments? Could not the military program be utilized? *(Respondent: Stanley Kronenberg)*

The mission of Civil Defense and the military differ significantly, and consequently their requirements for radiological instrumentation differ in many respects.

First, the military is concerned mainly with the effects of small, *tactical* weapons for battlefield use. The radius of total destruction of such weapons is smaller than the range of their initial nuclear radiation (INR) (gamma rays and fast neutrons). Both radiation components are delivered at extremely high dose rates and are followed by fallout which delivers the gamma dose at moderate dose rates. Each radiation component (of the INR) contributes about equally to the total dose to personnel.

In contrast, Civil Defense must deal with *strategic* nuclear weapons such as might be used by an enemy on targets within the continental United States. The radius of total destruction produced by these weapons exceeds the range of the INR, and only radiation and contamination produced by fallout are of radiological consequence. Therefore, tactical military dosimeters must be more sophisticated than those for Civil Defense. A tactical dosimeter must measure the total dose in mixed gamma/neutron fields and must not suffer from dose rate saturation at even the highest observable radiation intensities. Civil Defense dosimeters are expected to function only for gamma rays at fallout dose rates (below several thousand rads per hour).

Second, unit cost of instruments is an important factor. The Civil Defense effort has to protect over 200 million people in the U.S., and therefore the Civil Defense radiological instruments must be highly cost-effective. The military is concerned with the battlefield with a much lower number of participants where the unit cost factor is less important.

Third, reliability is important for both Civil Defense and the military; but while the military maintenance and calibration of instrumentation are well organized, Civil Defense instruments are often in the hands of civilians, where maintenance is expected to be poor. A Civil Defense dosimeter or ratemeter may be expected to remain forgotten without periodic calibration or maintenance for very long times but must be available and operational in the case of emergency. This special reliability is required for Civil Defense instrument design.

Fourth, power source requirements differ. The military does not mind using batteries which must be periodically removed, but battery replacement results in grave logistic problems for Civil Defense. Therefore, preferably, Civil Defense instruments should not depend on any electrical power source.

For these reasons, it is evident that the development of instruments for Civil Defense and for the military must be separate. In reality, however, it is not quite the case. There is a very close cooperative exchange of information and mutual support between the military services and the Federal Emergency Management Agency (FEMA) in the development of radiological instrumentation. An example is the utilization of radiochromic waveguide dosimetry. The developmental principle of this was financed by FEMA but was a joint technical effort of FEMA, the National Bureau of Standards and Army scientists. The resulting approach is a very versatile system which should result in a very inexpensive, durable and unsophisticated but reliable Civil Defense dosimeter: a 10 cm long, 3 mm diameter piece of radiochromic waveguide becomes discolored by gamma rays in the dose range between 10 and 1,000 rads. This permanently changed color can be read using ambient light by comparing it with a translucent strip of plastic with a built-in color scale (calibrated in tissue rads). The same general principle is utilized to read dose in the sophisticated Army wrist-watch radiac. Here a system of waveguides is read electronically to obtain the doses of gammas and neutrons from both INR and fallout. A microprocessor evaluates these readings and displays real-time dose information.

Both of the above instruments are in their research stage.

It is understood that the Army and Civil Defense radiation instrument development programs have for many years been closely coordinated. Based on this experience, what do you see coming up in Civil Defense instrumentation? *(Respondent: Stanley Kronenberg)*

Two instrument types in particular seem to me to offer great promise. They are a low cost ionization chamber dosimeter and charger, and a dosimeter based on a radiochromic waveguide.

The Low-Cost 200 R Dosimeter and Charger

This all-plastic dosimeter functions on the ion chamber principle. The dosimeter resembles the well known "fountain pen dosimeters" and works on the same principle. An ion chamber is initially charged electrically and ionization discharges it. The amount of discharge is proportional to the dose and is read with a fiber electrometer. The new version of this device was designed by FEMA. Its plastic construction results in superior quantum energy independence and lower cost. The platinized quartz fiber of the electrometer was replaced by the much more rugged and reliable carbon fiber. The insulator between the electrodes of the ion chamber (Cerex 250, preferred formula) has a very high resistivity and eliminates all visible charge leakage. Therefore, the instrument can read doses down to the background level. The dosimeter is activated by charging it by means of a piezoelectric charger which does not need any power source or maintenance and is easy and convenient to operate.

The combination of a low range version of this dosimeter and its charger, together with a watch, can be used as a very inexpensive durable and reliable dose rate meter. After being charged, one measures the time needed to obtain a noticeable discharge and thus computes the dose rate.

The Radiochromic Waveguide

This device offers possibilities for a very low cost Civil Defense dosimeter. It is expected not only to be inexpensive but also durable and maintenance free. It consists of a five-sided box approximately 4 x 3 x 2 cm made of black plastic. The wall opposite the open end has a slot through which a strip of transparent color scale can be inserted. This scale, which is calibrated in rads, can be moved back and forth in front of a series of holes drilled in the plastic. The user sees a row of spots of different color intensity. Below the center scale hole is another opening in which a radiochromic waveguide is inserted. Exposure to radiation changes the color until the center-scale-hole matches the color seen through the waveguide in the hole below. The dose is read on the edge of the scale. Ambient room light is used to read this dosimeter. The scale can be rolled up and stored in the dosimeter together with the waveguide resulting in a compact package. Several waveguides with different sensitivity ranges may be used to expand the dynamic range of this device.

Do you think a true "wrist-watch" type all-purpose radiation measuring instrument will become available, and if so when? *(Respondent: Stanley Kronenberg)*

It will not be available in the *near* future. However, a wrist-watch radiac is a proposed Army device. In addition to being a wrist-watch, it combines a tactical dosimeter with a tactical dose ratemeter and thus provides real-time data on the radiological status of the troops. To fulfill its purpose, it must measure all components of the tactical nuclear environment which consists of prompt initial gamma rays, prompt initial neutrons and fallout gammas. Recent progress in microelectronics make the circuitry for such an instrument possible, but the state-of-the-art of detectors had to be advanced to meet the requirements.

To measure the dose from the INR as well as the fallout gamma dose, radiochromic waveguide dosimeters were invented and developed. Optical waveguides are fabricated by filling plastic capillaries with a radiochromic substance which changes its transmissivity and its index of refraction by exposure to radiation. These changes are permanent and are independent of the exposure rate. The dose readout is accomplished with a built-in light source and a light detector. This system does not saturate at very high dose rates of the INR.

To measure the ambient fallout dose rates, GM tubes must be replaced by solid state counters, e.g., CdTe. To make them suitable for this application, we eliminated the effect of sensitivity changes caused in these devices by exposure to neutrons. This was accomplished by a compensating circuit which provides a constant output sensitivity regardless of the sensitivity of the detector.

The wris-watch radiac is expected to save dollars, save manpower, and minimize equipment size, weight and burden to the soldier. It should replace the following currently used instruments: AN/VDR-2, PP-4370, IM-185, and CP-696. The total savings is expected to be about 192 million dollars (FY 83 dollars) and 1620 man years over its 20-year cycle.

The wrist-watch radiac reduces the equipment weight from 22 kilograms to 85 grams and the volume from 16,000 cm^3 to 7 cm^3.

What are the new developments in Army radiological instruments? *(Respondent: Stanley Kronenberg)*

There are four new radiacs that will soon become available.

Radiacmeter IM-185

The IM-185 is a tactical dosimeter whose purpose is to provide the Commanding Officer instantly with data about the radiological status of his troops. It is capable of recording both gamma and neutron doses in rads from both the ultra-high dose rates INR or from radioactive fallout, radiological agents, or neutron-induced activity. It can be read directly at any time. It is a fountain-pen-size, quartz-fiber radiacmeter similar to the IM-93 but with a tissue equivalent plastic chamber operating in a vacuum on the SEMIRAD (Secondary Electron Mixed Radiation Dosimeter) principle. Primary electrons resulting from gamma radiation and recoil protons resulting from neutron radiation cause low-energy secondary electrons to be emitted from the walls of the plastic chamber. These secondary electrons are collected, causing the quartz-fiber electroscope to discharge, deflecting the image of the quartz-fiber on the electroscope scale. The instrument reads the total cumulative neutron and gamma dose, in rads (0-600), delivered to the tissue equivalent plastic chamber and is dose-rate independent. The dosimeter can be recharged to zero at any time as desired or required, by using the Detector Charger which replenishes the positive charge on the quartz-fiber. SEMIRAD neutron and gamma ray instrument have been successfully used to make basic measurements at nuclear-weapons tests.

AN/VDR-2

VDR-2 is a U.S. Army instrument (under development) for use in a nuclear fallout environment. It can perform ground radiological surveys either in vehicles or by individual soldiers as a hand-held instrument. It can also provide a quantitative measure of radiation to aid the decontamination of personnel, equipment and supplies. The major components of the AN/VDR-2 system are the radiacmeter and the probe, each of which contains a gamma sensing device (Geiger-Mueller tube). The AN/VDR-2 measures gamma dose rates from 0.02 mrad per hour (background) to 999 rads per hour. The dose rate is displayed on a three digital Liquid Crystal Display (LCD). The radiacmeter has the capability of time-integrating the dose rate counts and displaying the cumulative dose on command. The system is self-ranging. The unit is hand-carried by the soldier without the probe to measure high-level gamma dose rates and total dose. With the probe, the AN/VDR-2 detects beta and measures gamma contamination (at low dose rates) in equipment, supplies, personnel and food and water. Other features available are alarm setting and alarm check, audio-visual alarms, instrument and battery test, vehicle attenuation factor set, push to read external dose-rate and illumination of display. The instrument is powered by batteries or 28-volt vehicular power.

AN/ADR-6(V) Aerial Radiac System (ARS)

The ARS is radiation detecting equipment under development that is operated in U.S. Army aircraft for use during quick reaction special missions. The ARS is used for rapid aerial surveillance of large terrain contaminated by nuclear debris emitting gamma rays. Use of this equipment reduces the potential exposure of troops to radioactive contamination. It computes the ground dose rate using the dose rate at the aircraft and its altitude.

The ARS is composed of a detector, computer, power supply, control alarm indicator, recorder and a radar altimeter. During operation, gamma rays from contaminated ground areas strike the detector scintillator material producing light flashes. These are amplified by a photomultiplier tube where the output signal is applied to the logarithmic converter circuit board.

The computed gamma intensity on the ground is recorded on a built in strip chart recorder. From these recordings isodose-rate lines on the ground can be generated.

The operational range of this device is 0.04 to 400 rads per hour. It responds within the quantum energy range of 80 keV to 3 MeV.

Individual Dosimeter DT-236

This dosimeter will be worn by each individual soldier to provide the Army with the record of total cumulative gamma and neutron radiation doses to the troops. This device is currently entering production.

To detect gammas, it uses silver-activated phosphate glass. The neutron detector is a wide-base silicon junction diode. The range of this device is 1 to 1000 rads for both gammas and neutrons. Its accuracy is plus or minus 30 percent. It weighs 57 grams and has the shape of a wrist-watch which can be worn on the wrist or be attached to the dog tag.

To read the dose requires the Radiac Computer-Indicator CP-696. The reading is obtained by inserting the dosimeter in the reader. The reader weighs 10 kg and measures 30 x 20 x 20 cm. It operates with a BA-5590 lithium primary battery or with 120/240 volt, 50-60 Hz power. The combined fast neutron and gamma doses are read. The gamma portion of the reader measures the light emitted by the phosphate glass when exposed to ultraviolet radiation. This light output is proportional to the gamma dose. The neutron dose is obtained by measuring the resistance of the silicon diode.

Do the experiences of the Marshall Islanders prove that in the event of a nuclear war the major part of the United States would be so contaminated by radioactive fallout that continued habitation would be impossible? *(Respondent: Ed Lessard)*

I plan to answer this by explaining the important events in the Marshall Islands and relating them to the expected levels of radiation from a nuclear war in which a major part of the United States is contaminated.

Persons who were present on March 1, 1954, at Rongelap Island, Rongelap Atoll, Sifo Island, Ailingnae Atoll, and Utirik Island, Utirik Atoll in the Marshall Islands have been examined by medical specialists to determine if any observable effects occurred as a result of exposure to radioactive fallout from the Pacific weapon test known as Operation Castle BRAVO. Medical specialists have reported short-term effects exhibited over a period of many months and possible long-term effects exhibited over many years. A study was undertaken to re-examine dose estimates for people who were exposed accidentally at Rongelap, Sifo, and Utirik Islands.

The original estimates of external whole-body dose from the acute exposure were 1.75 Gy (175 rad) at Rongelap and 0.14 Gy (14 rad) at Utirik (Cronkite, Bond, and Dunham, 1956). The first estimate of thyroid dose from internal emitters in Rongelap people was 1.0 to 1.5 Gy (100 to 150 rad). Thus, the first estimate of total thyroid absorbed dose was 2.68 to 3.15 Gy (268 to 315 rad) for Rongelap people in general and for internal plus external exposure.

In 1964, three teenage girls who were exposed in 1954 underwent surgery for benign thyroid nodules. In 1964, 3- to 4-year-old child thyroid dose was re-examined by James on the basis of (1) urine bioassay results, and (2) a range of values for thyroid burden of ^{131}I, thyroid mass, and uptake retention functions for iodine (James, 1964). In addition, two modes of intake were considered, inhalation and ingestion. For 3- to 4-year-old girls the extreme range of thyroid dose from internal emitters was estimated at 2 to 33 Gy (200 to 3300 rad). The most probable total thyroid dose was in the range of 7 to 14 Gy (700 to 1400 rad). The James estimate of most probable total thyroid absorbed dose to the child was two to five times higher than the estimate reported by Cronkite for Rongelap people.

The conclusion of our 1984 acute exposure study was that the population mean thyroid absorbed dose at Rongelap was 21 Gy (2,100 rad). It was 6.7 Gy (670 rad) at Sifo and 2.8 Gy (280 rad) at Utirik (Lessard et al., 1984a). The major route for intake of fallout was by direct ingestion. This resulted from outdoor food preparation and consumption practices during the period fallout clouds passed over the islands. These are the highest estimates of mean thyroid dose reported. The original estimates of external whole-body dose were in agreement with our 1984 estimates.

A significant medical conclusion is that mortality of the exposed people is not different from a sex-and-age-matched comparison group of Marshall Islanders. Two cases of thyroid ablation occurred at Rongelap shortly after the 1954 acute exposure. Thyroid cancer and thyroid nodules occurred with greater frequency in the exposed people. Thyroid lesions required medical treatment and followup in order to prevent complications. Eight out of 251 exposed people have experienced thyroid cancer, whereas only two cases were expected. Skin lesions and depilation, which occurred within a few weeks after March 1, 1954, cleared up within a year and could have been serious without medical care.

Some warning of fallout would be available to U.S. citizens and the fallout may be visible. There is some time for evasive action. Outside of an area of blast and thermal damage, many water and power systems and fallout shelters may be essentially intact. Avoiding contact with fallout, wearing clothes, and taking shelter for a few weeks would reduce thyroid, skin and whole-body doses below thresholds for serious non-stochastic effects.

The peak exposure rate at Rongelap was 6.5 mC kg^{-1} h^{-1} (25 R h^{-1}). Rongelap people maintained their routine outdoor living pattern for two days after March 1, 1954, and were then evacuated. A shelter with a protection factor of 40 could have reduced their external whole-body doses below 0.05 Gy (5 rad). By avoiding the ingestion of dust for the first two days, they would have allowed the short-lived thyroid-seeking nuclides to decay away, greatly reducing their thyroid dose.

In order to extrapolate to future potential post-war conditions, the Rongelap exposure experience was expanded to four days and assumed to begin at one hour post detonation. The U.S. average exposure rate predicted by Jack Greene for a particular hypothesized attack was estimated to be about 130 mC kg^{-1} h^{-1} (500 R h^{-1}) at one hour post detonation if all the fallout had arrived by that time. A shelter that would provide a reduction of exposure rate by a factor of 40 would reduce this one hour rate to 3.2 mC kg^{-1} h^{-1} (12.5 R h^{-1}). The in-shelter four-day exposure based on standard decay (an exposure that often is used to compare fallout delivered exposures with acutely delivered exposures) would be 9.5 mC kg^{-1} (37 R). Rapid decline in exposure rate, greater than standard decay, was observed at Rongelap because of the presence of short-lived transuranics and activation products in BRAVO fallout. The in-shelter four-day exposure based on BRAVO fallout decline ($t^{-1.4}$) would be 6.7 mC kg^{-1} (26 R). If skin contact and ingestion of fallout dust could be avoided, then thyroid ablation and skin lesions would be avoided as well. Thus, it is conceivable that shelters would offer significant protection against over-exposure to fallout radiation and fallout dust.

I chose 130 mC kg^{-1} h^{-1} (500 R h^{-1}) for projection because it was a hypothetical average U.S. land-area-weighted and standardized value. The unweighted upper range was 85 mC kg^{-1} h^{-1} (330 R h^{-1}) for 1 percent of U.S. land area. Thus, based on BRAVO fallout decline, and initiating exposure at one hour, I estimate the upper range value to be associated with an in-shelter four-day exposure of 44 mC kg^{-1} (170 R). This value is similar to the unsheltered exposure received by people at Rongelap.

Exposure at Rongelap had in fact begun at five hours and ended at 53 hours post detonation. Arrival times greater than one hour might be expected for most areas unaffected by direct weapons effects. This time delay would reduce exposure projections given in the above examples. Rongelap was about one hundred miles from the BRAVO fallout cloud shortly after the detonation and the cloud moved at an average rate of 20 mph, which is very typical of wind speeds at the upper air levels.

In order to avoid unwarranted external and internal dose from the surface radioactivity, the inhabitants of Rongelap, Sifo, and Utirik were relocated out of the affected areas. They returned to Utirik in June 1954 and to Rongelap in June 1957. Environmental and personnel radiological monitoring programs were initiated in the mid-1950s by Brookhaven National Laboratory. The objective was to maintain a comprehensive radiological safety program. The dosimetric conclusions for the protracted exposure are summarized in Table E (Lessard et al., 1984b).

Table E. Dosimetric Conclusions for the Protracted Exposure of Rongelap and Utirik Adults from Day of Return to 50 Years. Table entries are committed effective dose equivalent (mSv) ± 1 S.E.

Nuclide	Rongelap	Utirik
^{55}Fe	0.48 ± 0.25 mSv	0.36 ± 0.20
^{60}Co	0.34 ± 0.13	0.44 ± 0.33
^{65}Zn	1.9 ± 1.0	30. ± 44.
^{90}Sr	0.53 ± 0.80	0.10 ± 0.05
^{137}Cs	22. ± 11.	13. ± 10.
External	17. ± 3.4	41. ± 8.2

Aside from Rongelap and Utirik resettlement, another protracted exposure experience was followed by us. From the mid-1940s through 1958, the U.S. conducted high-yield weapons tests at Bikini and Enewetak Atolls. These areas were contaminated with fallout from the tests. A restoration program, concentrating on the main residence islands of Bikini and Eneu Islands at Bikini Atoll, began in 1969. The Bikini population increased to some 140 individuals at the time of their departure in August 1978.

From the period 1974 to 1978, the Bikini people exhibited ever increasing body burdens of ^{137}Cs and ^{90}Sr. Based on the intake pattern exhibited by adults, we established a committed dose equivalent of 8.4 mSv (0.84 rem) from internally deposited ^{137}Cs, 2.0 mSv (0.20 rem) from ^{90}Sr and 0.032 mSv (0.0032 rem) from ^{60}Co.

External radiation exposure at Bikini (minus natural background) was 5.5 mSv (0.55 rem). The average time the exposed adults were at Bikini Atoll was 4.5 years. The people were removed to Kili Island in August 1978, and we are anticipating further cleanup activities at Bikini Atoll.

The ratio of total internal committed effective dose equivalent to external dose equivalent for protracted exposure was plotted by us versus time and return relative to the BRAVO detonation. It is apparent to us that the ratio increases with increasing time post return. The ratio was 1.1 at Utirik for people who returned after three months, 1.5 for Rongelap people who returned after three years and 2.0 for Bikini people who returned after 20 years. The major event contributing radioactivity to these locations was the BRAVO test.

Keeping committed organ dose equivalents below 500 mSv (50 rem) in one year should be sufficient to avoid non-stochastic effects. If the exposure rate is 130 mC kg h^{-1} (500 R h^{-1}) at one hour post detonation, this below-50-rem-in-one-year guide will be met for unsheltered conditions beginning at 30 months after the war. I assumed the gamma decay exponent to be -1.2 and the internal to external ratio to be 1.5. Thus, during the first two-and-one-half years, people will have to spend part of the time in shelters in order to keep committed organ doses equivalents below 500 mSv (50 rem).

During the first five years after the fallout arrived at Rongelap, the gamma decay exponent was -1.7. This would lead us to estimate an earlier departure time from shelter. Significant man-made and natural alterations to the source of radioactivity would also lead to early departure from shelter.

The increased average excess frequency of cancer mortality due to protracted radiation exposure was estimated to be two to four percent, that is, a 12 to 25 percent increase in the spontaneous rate from 30 months out to the end of life. An additional residual risk of cancer mortality would be anticipated from the acute exposure. If the whole-body dose during the first four months is at 3.0 gray (300 rad), then an additional excess frequency of 1.5 to 3 percent would be estimated. Greater doses delivered over shorter periods of time increase the likelihood of non-stochastic effects, and this alters our estimate of future stochastic effects. A range of risk is estimated because stochastic effects are protracted in time and their expression would be dependent upon the number of years remaining in the average survivor's life-span.

In summary, our conclusion, which is supported by the Marshall Islands experience, is that, in some areas of the United States, people either would have to spend essentially full time in shelters for weeks to months or they would have to be relocated to safer areas. In other parts of the country, shorter shelter stay-times would be required, and in some other areas, no special shelters would be needed. Even in the more highly contaminated areas after several years, remaining full time outside the shelters would not produce non-stochastic effects. Cancer incidence would be slightly greater than the spontaneous rate; however, other problems would likely be of greater concern to survivors.

Do you think that the survivors of a nuclear attack would possess the will to live, or would the survival problems appear so overwhelming that people simply would give up, not make the effort to continue, and perhaps kill themselves? *(Respondent: Howard Maccabee, M.D.)*

There seems to be a very popular idea that after a nuclear war or under a nuclear disaster the survivors would "envy the dead," i.e., that people would rather die or even commit suicide rather than continue to live after being subjected to the nuclear weapon effects. This idea has been trumpeted very broadly across the United States by the personality, Dr. Helen Caldicott, and some other members of Physicians for Social Responsibility, as well as by other groups, such as Educators for Social Responsibility.

Personally, I believe this idea is entirely fallacious.

There are several forms of evidence for my belief. First, in all of past history, there are almost no incidences whatsoever of people after a war disaster committing suicide. In fact, most of them fought on all the harder for survival. They tried to protect their families and to make a new life out of whatever was left when the war or the battle or the disaster was over.

Obviously, there are events in history such as Masada when a group of highly religious people committed suicide rather than be captured by the Romans to be made slaves or taken advantage of sexually or to lose their religious freedom. But that is an entirely different story from committing suicide or choosing not to live after surviving a major stressful episode.

Another form of evidence for my contention that people will always try to survive, no matter what has happened, is medical experience. I am a radiation oncologist, which means my specialty is cancer. Over the last few years, I have treated over eight hundred cancer patients. In a person's life, or in the family in which it occurs, the experience of cancer, especially if it is a cancer that is not cured, is just as stressful on an individual basis as the event of a nuclear disaster. To my knowledge, of the eight hundred cancer patients that I have treated and that have experienced this stress and this grief, there has been only one suicide. The great majority of people, no matter what they have to go through to survive, will fight with every ounce of strength and with every breath to go on living even if they can maintain only a semblance of a quality of life.

I believe this has been the experience of other oncologists and of other physicians in general.

It is my strong belief that most people *would not* give up their lives willingly after surviving the initial stages of a natural or a man-made disaster, including nuclear war.

What effect would the mass fires produced by nuclear attack have on the deposition of fallout and the subsequent radiation dose rates produced thereby? *(Respondent: Stan Martin)*

There is no doubt that an effect can result. I have a problem, though, deciding how significant the practical consequences may be.

Some experimental evidence exists, but it is very limited. Broido and McMasters modeled the effect on airborne particles in a 6-by-6-ft., low-velocity wind tunnel (Broido and McMasters, 1959). Perturbations in fallout patterns caused by a small gas-fed fire were pronounced. Unfortunately, this was not repeated on a more realistic scale. Lane and Lee made use of one of the large-scale fires on the FLAMBEAU program to investigate the redistribution of already deposited fallout simulant (Lane and Lee, 1968). They found that the fire-induced winds at ground level are quite sufficient to carry away fallout deposits. At least one analytical study (Miller and Strom at URS) has shown the reasonableness of such effects and a sense of what to expect.

So what? In a single-burst situation, any fallout produced should be long gone before a firestorm can develop (if indeed a firestorm is possible at all); so, perhaps this potential interaction pertains only to multiburst attacks. Even then, however, coincidence of the fallout and fire, in both time and location, requires several things to happen. First, a mass fire must result from one of the explosions. Second, the fallout cloud to be affected by the fire must come from a separate up-wind nuclear explosion (but not so far upwind that the fallout cloud has become widely, thinly dispersed by the time of interaction). Third, the two explosions must be time-sequenced appropriately to put the fallout cloud from one explosion in the *near vicinity* of the site of the other during the interval (i.e., a few hours) of its mass-fire activity, if any. I have not tried to work out the joint probability of these events occurring just as required, but I know the independent probability of the first--if mass fire is equated to firestorm--is so small that I must wonder if this is really a "non-problem." Even allowing that less intense, but extensive fires may produce a qualitatively similar result, the joint probability is still quite small.

For a straight answer, though, there seems to be a potentially beneficial effect. The limited evidence suggests that convective updrafts of fires can reduce the local and downwind deposition (density) of fallout, or at least delay its deposition and allow it to move further downwind. Actually, two effects are expected: (1) the updraft carries particles to greater heights to delay their final deposition and to lengthen their trajectories, allowing greater dispersion and more time for radioactive decay to reduce doses after the fallout reaches the ground; and (2) fire-induced turbulence further enhances disposition. The Broido and McMasters experiments lacked the turbulence of a large-scale fire, which may account for the displaced "hot spot" in their fallout patterns that is not predicted analytically. In a fully turbulent fire of large extent, the net effect on a fallout cloud would be expected to reduce the overall density of deposition, extending it further downwind. There is no reason to expect hot spots to result. What, if any, practical consequences would result from this, and how likely it is to occur at all, I am at this time unable to evaluate; but, the biggest uncertainty seems due to the still unresolved question of whether, and if so, how often, mass fires would result from nuclear explosions (Defense Nuclear Agency et al., 1985)

The comment is often heard that anyone caught in a mass fire situation (in the nuclear war context) would inevitably perish. Is this in accord with the experience of World War II and any other sources of insight? *(Respondent: Stan Martin)*

Many people caught in a fire situation would perish, whether or not it was a mass fire. But the statement often heard implies that nuclear explosions would turn whole cities into firestorms of the Hamburg type, and then survival would be impossible. This is an erroneous notion in several respects.

First, firestorms are a very unlikely result of nuclear explosions, even of airbursts of megaton yield. Neither American nor Soviet cities are of sufficient built-up densities, except possibly the central business downtowns of a few of the largest of them, to support a firestorm. Besides, nuclear explosions superimpose heavy blast damage on pretty much the same areas of a city as they set alight. Collapsed structures do not burn with the intensity needed for firestorm genesis, while in the periphery of this area of blast destruction, which can extend a long way out from ground zero, fires tend to be few and far between. Of course, the term "few" is relative. It means that only a small fraction of buildings are initially on fire, perhaps only one per city block, or 100 per square mile. Obviously, in an area of many square miles, that is a lot of fires, but not a firestorm threat, by any criterion accepted by the technical community.

Second, survival rates were surprisingly high in the firestorms of World War II. The reports emphasized the terrible loss of life--and it was terrible in both numbers of people and its ruthless disregard for age, sex, and innocent indifference to the motives of the Allied onslaught--and the futility, in some cases, of the measures taken for civilian protection, such as bomb shelters. Terrible as it was, loss of life in the firestorm areas averaged only some 12 to 15 percent of the population at risk, and never exceeded 20 percent. This is to be compared with five percent fatality rates in the burned-over areas of German cities that did not experience firestorms. Hiroshima is often said to have suffered a firestorm following the nuclear attack on that city, but neither the intensity of the fire nor casualty rates due to fire are comparably as large as the estimates for Hamburg, Dresden, and other German firestorm cities. Fatalities due to fire in Hiroshima were estimated at less than three percent of the population at risk, and the fire severity was estimated to be less than in the firestorm events in Germany by more than an order of magnitude.

Third, good fire protection for direct effects survivors can be provided with some effort (see Waterman's contribution in this regard). Much of the heavy loss of fire in World War II was avoidable had the warnings been heeded (Rumpf, 1931; Rumpf, 1952). I hope we will not repeat the mistake, and choose to ignore the lesson history teaches.

In the event of a nuclear attack on this country, will the fallout radiation produce immune depression severe enough to cause widespread disease and infections? *(Respondent: Fred Mettler)*

Overall, it is clear that radiation can affect the immune response. In situations in which the radiation dose is high enough to cause a "hematopoietic syndrome," there is decreased immune competence, as well as bleeding and anemia. In such severe situations, infection undoubtedly is one of the factors that contribute to the death of the individual. In situations in which the whole body dose is less than about one Gy (100 rad), the immune depression is unlikely to be a clinical problem in humans. A whole-body absorbed dose above this level, but below the lethal level, will produce a transient immune depression which will last less than two months.

Studies of the effects of whole body radiation on the immune system in humans are limited. Localized exposures, the presence of malignancy in radiotherapy situations, and the well-recognized normal decrease in immunocompetence associated with aging confound most available data. The major and best understood cell type involved in the immune function is the lymphocyte. Lymphocytes are involved in recognition of the foreign substance (antigen); induction and regulation of the immune response; the causing of the immune response to be very specific; and finally, responsibility for immunological memory.

Lymphocytes can be divided into two major subcategories on the basis of function. These two categories are "thymus" derived (T) cells, and bone marrow or "bursa" (B) cells. The two classes do not work completely independently. There is major cooperation between T and B cells. The immune response itself can be divided into two broad categories: cellular and humoral. Cellular immunity is mediated by the T cells, and it is important in the process of rejection of incompatible grafts, graft vs. host disease, and delayed hypersensitivity responses. The humoral response is that of antibody synthesis, and the B cells are primarily responsible for this type of immunity, which is manifest by the production of immunoglobulins.

Early experiments demonstrated the marked radiosensitivity of small lymphocytes. Doses as low as 20 to 40 mGy (2 to 4 rads) cause significant alterations in motility and morphology of human lymphocytes irradiated and maintained *in vitro*. With radiation doses in the lethal range, changes in the small lymphocytes are so rapid that they can be found within an hour. Within three days, lymphoid tissues subjected to high doses of radiation may be almost completely devoid of lymphocytes.

Depression of the immune response following radiation is primarily due to the radiosensitivity of most small lymphocytes, and the major consequence of the immune suppression is increased susceptibility to infection, although an increase in the induction rate of neoplasms is also possible. When the radiation dose is delivered at a reduced dose rate, the radiation is much less effective in producing immune depression. This may be due to some repair of the radiation damage which occurs during either extended or fractionated exposures.

Overall, evidence indicates that B lymphocytes show more acute and rapid advancement of radiation injury than T lymphocytes. Restoration of the immune response is generally proportional to the absorbed dose received. After low dose exposures, regeneration may occur via the proliferation of the local, less radiosensitive cells. Following larger doses, regeneration is probably more importantly performed by repopulation from exogenous stem cells rather than proliferation of resistant small lymphocytes. With the larger doses, repopulation is delayed by nine to fourteen days, probably due to the maturation that the stem cell must undergo either in the thymus or in the bone marrow.

There have been several studies in humans that examine immunoglobulin levels following total body irradiation. One study included only 13 exposed persons and 46 unexposed controls. Minimal reductions in immunoglobulin (IgA and IgG) were reported. The small numbers of patients examined and problems in dose estimates make it difficult to assess the importance of these minimal findings. Patients therapeutically exposed to total body gamma irradiation at dose levels between 1 and 3.5 Gy (100-350 rads) also showed a reduction in IgA, IgM, and IgG. Immunoglobulin levels returned to close to normal by seven weeks following total body therapeutic irradiation. The order of decreasing sensitivity to irradiation is IgA, IgM and IgG.

Since the thymus is involved with the maturation phase of T lymphocytes, irradiation of the thymus might be expected to lead to profound effects. Data on exposure of the human thymus comes from persons accidentally exposed, as well as those undergoing radiation therapy. The data confirm the marked radiosensitivity of the lymphocytes within the human thymus. Multiple late effects have occurred as a result of therapeutic (high dose) localized irradiation of the thymus. There was an increased frequency of many uncommon diseases with immunological overtones such as sarcoid, thyroiditis and collagen diseases, and persistent depression of T cells among the irradiated group. T cell depression has been noted following chest wall irradiation of carcinoma of the breast. In these cases, the thymus was exposed to a dose estimated between 20 and 24 Gy (2,000 to 2,400 rads). Many studies have confirmed decreased immunocompetence following localized radiotherapy for a variety of tumors. It is unlikely that this sort of irradiation would occur in a fallout situation.

The immune function has been studied in the atomic bomb survivors, since it was demonstrated that peripheral chromosomal aberrations were present and that there was an increase in cancer incidence. The proportion of T cells in the peripheral lymphocytes of the heavily exposed survivors was not affected by radiation dose. Lymphocyte function, however, was demonstrated to be affected in terms of response to mitogen. Whether this is responsible for the increase in malignant tumors in the population is not known. The possibility of increased susceptibility to infection has been studied; no evidence has been found of the antibody EB virus as a function of radiation dose (Mettler, Jr. and Moseley, Jr., 1985). It does appear that the children who received heavy *in utero* exposures did have a temporary decrease in antibody-producing competence.

How does the American public view Civil Defense?
(Respondent: Jiri Nehnevajsa)

For three decades, there has existed a persistent and robust public support for efforts to help protect our people against the hazards of nuclear war: that is, for programs of Civil Defense. The "robustness" manifests itself by noting that favorable responses characterize the sentiments of between 60 and 90 percent of Americans, depending on the specific type of program or effort the respondents are asked to consider. The fact that strong opposition against *any* kind of Civil Defense has remained in the range of some eight to twelve percent only underscores the "robustness" of public support. The "persistency" of the results, in turn, can be easily shown by recognizing that the basic empirical indices have displayed remarkable stability across a time span of more than a quarter of a century.

Thus, for instance, 81.5 percent of the respondents (Sindlinger Poll, August 1982) agreed that the federal government has a *responsibility* to "provide protection for our people"; not that Civil Defense might somehow be "nice" to have, or that it "ought" to be "considered." Rather, it is seen as the government's *responsibility*.

Subtle differences do exist in patterns of approval of varying fundamental programs, such as public or private fallout sheltering, the need for blast shelters, or crisis relocation. However, the differences in the level of support tend to be consistently quite small. Thus, our people seem unwilling, or unable, to draw sharp distinctions among major classes of protective postures and are reluctant to render differentiated judgments about alternative *technical* and *organizational* means by which the desired enhanced protection might come about.

An interpretive explanation of these high levels of Civil Defense support may be provided along a good number of empirically grounded lines. In this very brief discussion, only three major factors are highlighted: the likelihood of nuclear war; the possible effects of Civil Defense on war likelihood; and perceptions of likely effectiveness, in terms of survival chances, of various major Civil Defense options. The threat of war, indeed, has been a very credible one throughout this historical period. At this time the public attaches a bit less than a fifty-fifty chance to the possibility of a nuclear conflagration, with modal responses placing such a conflict, were it ever to occur, within about a 10- to 20-year time frame.

However, in this regard, some important changes in the nation's thinking have taken place. High war expectations of the 1950s gave way to declining likelihood estimates throughout the 1960s and into the very early 1970s. Since about the mid-1970s, the likelihood indices have been on the rise again and have, as of late, reached again the relatively high levels of the "cold war" era of the 1950s.

Only some three to six percent of those surveyed, throughout these decades, have tended to argue that nuclear war would *never* happen. The central message of the findings is straightforward enough and its inherent logic somewhat difficult to deny:

The possibility of nuclear war cannot be ruled out. Thus, *some* measures are desirable, even though their specific technical nature may be impossible to properly evaluate, to be reasonably prepared if the unwanted worst should ever actually happen. Furthermore, the Federal Government ought to do the doing; it is, after all, its *responsibility*.

Our people, furthermore, *reject* the argument that Civil Defense would *increase* the likelihood of nuclear war. In fact, most consider the likelihood of war to be unaffected by Civil Defense programs one way or the other. Among the minority who do believe that war probabilities *are* sensitive to Civil Defense measures, *benign* efforts (*decreasing* war chances) are seen to exceed the more malignant consequences by a factor of about 2.5 to 3.

The strategic pattern of the findings is not modified whether one postulates that the Soviets might view our enhanced Civil Defense efforts as "provocative," or whether one considers the possibility that the nation's leadership might become more "trigger-happy" or reckless (on the truly obscene premise of some Civil Defense opponents that an American President might be prone to risk a nuclear war "*if only*" 50 million of our people were killed but not do so if 150 million were to perish!).

What are seen as the main purposes of having a Civil Defense program? Here, the nation's views depend on whether one asks about government's rationale for Civil Defense or the public's, as shown in Table F.

Table F. Perceived Reasons for Civil Defense. Table entries are in percent.

	Government's Rationale*	General Public's Rationale**
To save lives	32.3 ⎱ 55.3	47.7 ⎱ 63.7
Both to save lives and contribute to deterrence	23.0 ⎰	16.0 ⎰
	⎱ 54.7	⎱ 39.2
Contribute to deterrence	31.7 ⎰	23.2 ⎰
[None]	[3.6]	[5.4]
[Don't know, no answer]	[9.4]	[7.7]

*Gallup Study, June, 1982
**Gallup Study, October, 1982.

This means:

The Government is seen as seeking to balance the overall national *defense* needs and the life-saving potential in its main reasons for "keeping civil defense." For the nation's public, the life-saving potential is a significantly more important consideration (by a factor of 1.6) than is the possible role of Civil Defense as an aspect of overall defense. And only some four to five percent of the respondents believed that Civil Defense programs would neither help in saving lives nor contribute to deterrence.

There is, in fact, somewhat more to that as well. Some 59.8 percent believe that "Civil Defense plans for nuclear attack" would either "help very much" or "help somewhat" in coping with other disasters. In turn, 29.7 percent expressed themselves in saying that such plans would "help very little" or "not at all;" and 4.6 percent said that this would all depend on the "type of plans" (with an additional 6.0 percent of "don't knows" in this Gallup Study of August and September 1982).

To sum up:

Our people express the view that the nation would be better off in saving lives with, rather than without, Civil Defense should nuclear war actualize. The nation can, furthermore, also do somewhat better with, than without, Civil Defense in helping to prevent a war. And Civil Defense measures against the possible (and credible) threat of war also would have a significant payoff in the nation's ability to cope with other major emergencies.

If the potential for saving lives is considered, by the public, as the cornerstone of Civil Defense, how many lives might such measures actually save? Simply put: our people think that survivability rates would about *double* with prudent Civil Defense programs, as contrasted with a "next week's war" situation (when our protective measures for the population remain all but absent).

This is certainly no wild optimism, and the data reveal none of the dreaded "complacency" with nuclear war that some of the Civil Defense opponents like to emphasize. This doubling of survivability estimates goes from some 31.5 percent ("next week's war") to percentages in the low 60s (with blast shelters seen performing best, fallout shelters next, and crisis relocation programs last among these broad classes of options).

The central theme of such findings then (this author's study, late 1978) is about as follows:

Given such modest survival enhancement estimates, the robust levels of Civil Defense support indicate that even such improvements in survivability as seem achievable are well worth the effort. The survival estimates themselves are good clues to perceived effectiveness, if of moderate magnitudes, of measures to protect our people.

Without attempting to even touch upon many other important findings (on willingness to relocate, on helping behavior, on home basement sharing, on willingness to volunteer and so on and so on), one more major pattern of results, perhaps, merits some highlighting (the author's study, late 1978). In general, the supporters of Civil Defense are also in strong favor of arms control agreements with the Soviets.

Our people do not see arms control efforts at odds with Civil Defense programs. Rather, they see them as entirely compatible, if different, ways to help protect our people as well as to contribute to defusing to some extent the risks of nuclear war.

There are, perhaps, some important lessons in the persistent findings about the dispositions of our people. Only at great possible peril to the nation can such lessons be ignored, or their relevance minimized.

What impact, if any, might publicity (by Carl Sagan and others) about the possible "nuclear winter" effect of a nuclear war have on public support for Civil Defense? *(Respondent: Jiri Nehnevajsa)*

I start with a few observations:

First, there are no empirical data as yet of which I am aware to shed direct light on this potentially quite important question. Thus, in addressing this issue, I cannot but be somewhat more on the speculative side than I generally prefer to be.

Second, I suggest that the publicity accorded the TTAPS-type speculations (Turco et al., 1983) has thus far not really reached the more general body politic as information to be somehow confronted, internalized and dealt with. Thus, I would be surprised if more than 10 to 15 percent of our people *at this time* know much, if anything, about the "nuclear winter" hypotheses.

Third, as the underlying input structure and the models themselves (along with the scenarios used in the TTAPS study) are subject to increasing expert critique (some of which has already pointed to the significant effects on the model outputs of the model assumptions and of the host of uncertainties connected therewith -- some of them also recognized, though in a quite muted way, in the TTAPS materials themselves), the process is likely to attenuate some of the credibility of the nuclear winter hypothesis at least in its extreme form (as in Sagan's, and perhaps even more so, Paul Ehrlich's attempts at "popularization"). Be that as it may, however, it is not without value to assume wide-ranging publicity of the nuclear winter speculation and growing, though possible not really "massive" for some time, diffusion of such information throughout the nation's public. What then about Civil Defense?

As indicated above, in the absence of empirical evidence I will present several major speculations in the form of *hypotheses*: that is, assertions about the expected state of the world (effects of the nuclear winter speculation on public views regarding Civil Defense measures) which *can* be verified or rejected. In this response, I am not in a position to explain in a research-and-theory grounded manner why I suspect that these hypotheses are more likely to be verified rather than rejected once appropriate evidence is, or becomes, available.

Hypothesis 1

If our own, but above all the Soviet, Government(s) do not provide clear and unambiguous action clues that *they* consider the nuclear winter hypothesis a credible one, there will be essentially *no* effect on the persistent and prevailing favorable sentiments regarding the need for Civil Defense preparedness.

Such "clues" would have to be indicative of the conviction of the Governments, and especially -- to repeat -- of the Soviet one, that "nuclear war" would be suicidal in the sense that it has become truly impossible (even for the aggressor and even more the victim, ourselves, not to retaliate at all). Only *dramatic* agreements to reduce the strategic nuclear forces could serve as a reasonable signal that the Governments have concluded that a nuclear war actually *cannot* be fought at all (and this is different from the rhetoric that a nuclear war "cannot be won"). This is unlikely to happen in the near future if only because the TTAPS findings remain altogether tenuous on their own technical grounds.

Hypothesis 2

The eight to twelve percent of our people who have been consistently *opposed* to measures of Civil Defense, and whose views nothing appears to affect in the first place, are likely to be *reinforced* by the nuclear winter hypothesis, in the sense of having a "new" argument to present regarding the futility of doing anything at all. However, the persuasion efforts emanating from these individuals, and the issue-groups they occasionally form, have not affected the general public sentiments for three decades and I do not see that the nuclear winter speculation (providing, as it does, only some buttressing for the class of arguments made more qualitatively in Schell's *The Fate of the Earth* [Schell, 1982]) adds much to the effectiveness of the armamentarium of the Civil Defense antagonists.

Hypothesis 3

Were we to explain, even crudely, the kinds of post-nuclear attack conditions and ask our people whether they would be *likely* to survive a nuclear winter (a severe, perhaps even arctic period) were it to last as much as a year, we would get many "depends" type of answers. It would turn out that people would argue that their survival prospects would "depend" on availability of heat, food, medications, clothing, and so forth. Among the elderly and among people in ill health, the non-survival response would tend to be more dominant. Many (though not a majority, I think; the majority is most likely in the "depends" category) would, in effect, say: So what? Why would a one-year severe winter *not* be survivable? Of course we could "rough it" somehow and survive. Obviously, the underlying hypothesized pattern of response then itself is a function of the extent to which there might exist viable preparedness measures to facilitate survival even in a nuclear winter environment.

Along this axis, the nuclear winter hypothesis, for what it may be worth, does affect the kinds of Civil Defense *planning* that might be called for, especially with much more emphasis on the post-war situation over some relevant time horizon, and on planning involving possible "stockpiling" to affect the "depends" type of survivability response. That is to say, *our government's* response in the way of concepts, plans and preparedness systems to the "possible" nuclear winter postulation would be a crucial factor in determining public views regarding the possibility of coping even with that kind of a nightmarish predicament.

Hypothesis 4

If, in turn, we were to ask our people whether they would *try to survive* (rather than estimating their prospects for surviving), I would estimate that between 85 to 90 percent of our people would give an *unequivocal Yes* to such a question. Our people have not been known, either throughout the nation's history or its present, to be simple "quitters." And were we to ask whether, even if they personally might not live through the nightmare(s), they would *try to make survival possible* for their spouses, children, grandchildren, kinfolk, friends and neighbors, and even strangers, we are likely to get something on the order of 95 percent strong affirmative reactions.

Hypothesis 5

Were we to ask, explicitly, whether the Federal Government ought to invest manpower and resources which would enhance survivability, even under the nuclear winter speculation, by better plans, preparedness systems, stockpiling measures and what not, I would expect some 90 percent of our people to endorse such efforts in principle, though fewer would endorse them, perhaps by a factor of 0.6 to 0.7, if the "annual costs" seemed exorbitant (billions of dollars per year), and if such costs would have to be absorbed by cutting back on other domestic programs perceived as ones of high immediacy and high priority.

Hypothesis 6

I also expect some non-negligible percentage of our people (for the sake of argument, call it 15 to 20 percent) to be confused about the distinctions between nuclear winter and "Nuclear Freeze" concepts, much as they *now* are in considering "relocation" to mean evacuation from one's home to a nearby "shelter" rather than what "crisis relocation" is really about (the movement, on the order of 50 miles and more, *away* from probable high risk areas to probable lower/negligible risk areas of the country).

In sum, I do not see the nuclear winter speculation, no matter how well publicized and no matter how well diffused as "information" throughout our public, as degrading the prevailing patterns of support for programs and measures to prepare the nation to cope with *all* emergencies, including the "unthinkable" (as Herman Kahn phrased it years ago) threat of nuclear war.

One of these days, of course, actual data have to tell us their own story; I do not expect the data to lead to drastically different conclusions from those which I have stated in the preceding paragraphs.

Do you think that current fallout models as used in hypothetical attack analysis over- or under-predict average fallout radiation levels to be expected following a nuclear attack, or do you think they are about right? *(Respondent: Hillyer G. Norment)*

First, let us be sure to define our terms. My experience is mostly with local, prompt (H + 48 hr or less) fallout from single, isolated nuclear explosions. The nuclear winter hypothesis, hereafter referred to as TTAPS (Turco et al., 1983) is concerned with intermediate (H + 2 days to 1 month) fallout. Since I know most about the prompt fallout, I will discuss that first.

We should consider prediction of prompt fallout for two categories of explosions, low yield ($\lesssim 10$

kT) and high yield (≳1 MT). For low yields, we can quite adequately (to ~10-20 R/hr H + 1 hr dose rate) predict fallout activity from surface bursts, provided that we use a model that has low yield capability. The only such models that I know of are DELFIC, SIMFIC, and DNAF-1. This capability exists mostly because of the following:

- We can adequately simulate cloud rise.
- We can estimate adequate (ballpark) dust loading.
- We can distribute activity with particle size to account for fractionation.
- We have what seems to be good experimental data on fallout size distribution for Nevada Test Site fallout.

The last point is the critical one. The particle size distribution data were obtained from the few test shots that were properly instrumented to collect fallout over the extent of the close-in fallout fields. Prediction is very sensitive to the particle size distribution. For the high yield category, the situation is much different, and one can draw one's own conclusions from the following restrictions or limitations:

- We do not know the particle size distribution.
- We have no whole-pattern observations to compare predictions against.

Next, let us look at the models that are used for attack analyses. I am aware of two such models: WSEG-10 (Pugh and Galiano, WSEG-RM 10, 1959), which is used by the U.S. Department of Defense; and SEER (Lee, Wong and Brown, SRI, DNA 2962F, 1962), which is used by NATO. The older WSEG-10 model is much superior from a modeling perspective, and also is much simpler and faster. Both were designed primarily to predict for high yield (MT) cases. They both seriously over-predict for low yields. For high yield cases, which are of greatest interest, we simply do not know their accuracy.

I know of no past attempts, that I would take seriously, to predict intermediate fallout. I cannot critique the TTAPS work without thoroughly studying their models. I have looked at the dust input data in the TTAPS paper. The critical data, at least for the dust part of their calculations, are all presented and are quite reasonable. Also, their activity K factor (R/hr-mi^2/kT) (quoted by Jim Buchanan of the NCRP staff) is okay. This, along with the overall presentation of the TTAPS paper and a glance through a few of their references, indicate a high level of competence. On the other hand, they present only a cursory discussion of their gamma radiation dose results, with virtually no details on how they arrived at them. That their results are in accord with certain prior calculations is not convincing in and of itself.

It is a shame that fallout prediction also is in rather poor shape. I believe that the situation can be remedied, since I believe that models now can be developed that can calculate particle size distribution evolution in the fireball environment; there have been great advances in aerosol physics recently. Carl Miller made a modest beginning back in the days when modern tools were not available. Still, the work done by John Norman at Gulf Atomic, which was encouraged by Miller and supported by the Civil Defense Agency, would be of critical importance to such an effort.

Do you think the particle size distributions of the surface over which a bomb might be detonated--clay-type soils as opposed to the alluvial soils of the Nevada Test Site, or the coral surfaces in the Pacific--would affect the amount or distribution of the fallout radioactivity? *(Respondent: Hillyer G. Norment)*

With regard to sensitivity of predictions to various types of soils, I suspect that it may be substantial. Also, there can be no question about sensitivity to height of burst. But again, the available data are restricted to low yields, over alluvial type soils, and consist of the gross measure "fraction down" which does not give us what we need for modeling that can be used to provide credible predictions.

[Editor's Note: Thus, the fallout experience at the Nevada Test Site and in the Pacific tests, may lead to overestimates of fallout exposures from nuclear blasts over other locations. The particle sizes generated by a blast over a typical city would tend to be smaller and stay in the atmosphere longer. JCG]

Even if a person were lucky enough to survive the blast, thermal and fallout radiation effects of a nuclear attack, would he or she not sooner or later be doomed to die from a malignancy induced by the ionizing radiation to which he had been exposed? *(Respondent: Warren Sinclair)*

No. There would be a per capita increase in the number of deaths due to radiation-induced cancer, but this increase would not be large--only a few percent.

The risk of radiation-induced cancer, of course, depends on the doses of radiation to which the survivors of a nuclear attack are exposed. There is no means by which one realistically can predict what these exposures would be. A limit, on the one hand, would be essentially no exposure to those fortunate to be in an area not affected by fallout. The limit, on the other hand, is that most of those receiving acute doses above about 400 rad would not live long enough to develop cancers. The doses that survivors of an attack actually would receive depend on many variables, including the design of the attack (number of weapons, ground or air bursts, targeting, etc.) and on how well people were able to shelter themselves and how carefully they avoided excessive exposures after coming out of shelters.

Assume that the average dose for one group of survivors would be 100 rad and for another group, 200 rad. The United Nations Scientific Committee on the Effects of Atomic Radiation (UNSCEAR, 1977) gave risk estimates for low doses (a few rads at most), using a factor of 2.5 for dose reduction from the data at 100 rad to low doses. The mean for males and females was 1.25×10^{-4} per rad for total cancer mortality. The net incidence of cancer would be at least a factor of two higher.

For mortality at 100 rad or above, the factor of 2.5 should be put back, i.e., the risk is $2.5 \times 1.25 \times 10^{-4}$ per rad. At 100 rads, this is about three percent and at 200 rads about six percent. That is, three percent of the people exposed to 100 rad and six percent of the people exposed to 200 rad will get fatal cancer attributable to the exposures. A similar number of people will get a (presumably) curable cancer.

For perspective, according to the *1983 World Almanac*, in 1980 there were 1,986,000 deaths in the United States, of which 414,320 were caused by malignant neoplasms (cancers), or about 21 percent. If the 1980 lifestyle were to continue post-attack, including the same per capita consumption of cigarettes, the risk of dying from cancer for these two groups would go from 21 percent to 24 percent and to 27 percent, respectively.

Do U.S. mines and caves represent a practical resource for protecting our population in the event of a threat of a nuclear attack, and if so, what would you recommend be done now (before such a threat has arisen) to assure that this resource could be used effectively? *(Respondent: George Sisson)*

If all attempts to avoid a nuclear conflict came unravelled and we found ourselves facing such a situation, and if each of us could find a dry, level mine in which to take shelter, we could be highly confident that we could survive such conflict. Mines offer virtually complete protection against fallout and substantial protection against blast.

The first limited survey made for the purpose of using mines in a wartime context was made shortly after World War II with the idea of locating industrial installations underground. (Allied efforts to damage underground manufacturing plants had met with very limited success.) This 1946 U.S. Army Corps of Engineers survey located more than 400,000,000 square feet of highly desirable mine space, mostly in the northeast quadrant of the country. That survey is nearly 40 years old, and it was not complete. No one knows how much more good space might be available.

By 1961, when a national fallout shelter survey was undertaken, mines were recognized as high-quality candidates for providing fallout protection for the population, and were on the list of those facilities which were surveyed to determine their adequacy as fallout shelter. For a number of reasons, this survey, too, was very limited.

The desire to make use of mines for sheltering our population was an incentive for many follow-on studies. Slowly a number of facts emerged.

There was no complete inventory of all the mine space in the nation, nor was there an up-to-date record of the condition of the space.

With the realization that a nuclear war would be unlikely to occur "out of the blue," much more of the space which does exist could be used to shelter the people evacuated from likely target areas during a crisis.

Experimental studies showed that mines could be equipped expediently (in one or two days) with lighting and ventilation.

An unexpected finding was that mines offer superior protection against blast--because of their huge volume compared to the small access openings--and thus offer shelter in the higher risk areas.

With these facts in hand, it seems strange that the planning necessary to make use of this space in a crisis has not been undertaken. Mine space is far more effective than shoring up existing buildings and covering them with earth (although both options would be required in a national program.) Furthermore, it is the best space available and can be made ready for use with far less effort per person than can any other available option.

What is needed is a national survey, utilizing all available sources such as the U.S. Bureau of Mines, State Geological Surveys, etc., to determine the number, location, size, and condition of all existing mines. Those found unsuitable because of instability, existing gases, harmful bacteria, and wetness would be eliminated from a shelter list.

Next, the available space must be matched with the population which would be moved into those areas during a crisis, and as many people as possible assigned to the available mines.

Plans for use of the mines must include provisions for stringing up light bulbs powered by portable generating devices, and for ventilating the space. This can be done by bicycle-driven ventilation kits already developed, or by the provision of large electric fans installed at outlets, as was done in previous government research.

It is true that the upgrading of existing buildings is a very effective means of providing fallout protection in those areas where direct weapons effects are not likely. However, this method requires much more work and material. The use of mines as a first option not only makes sense as a high quality protection measure but also, on a national scale, could very significantly reduce the requirement to shore and cover existing buildings.

The idea of building in some measure of protection in new construction is practiced in some countries, particularly in Scandinavia--do you think this idea would make sense in the U.S., and if so, can you give rough estimates of: (a) the expected effectiveness of such measures; (b) the incremental costs in construction; and (c) how long such a program might take to "mature"? *(Respondent: George Sisson)*

The term "slanting" of structures to achieve nuclear weapons effects protection was coined by the Navy Bureau of Yards and Docks in the early days of full-scale nuclear weapons effects test programs. The main emphasis at that time was to "slant" or minimally alter design features, when designing a new structure, so as to strengthen certain parts of the building in order to incorporate a measure of blast and thermal protection while simultaneously providing all the normal features for everyday use. It was reasoned that direct effects protection could thus be developed at significantly smaller costs than would be necessary to provide a "blast" shelter solely to protect people in case of nuclear attack. At that time, the fallout threat was not widely understood, and thus the early emphasis was on direct weapons effects.

The idea remains attractive to the present day and was actively pursued (for fallout slanting) by the Office of Civil Defense in the early 1960s, when the major effort was to provide or locate shelter offering protection against fallout radiation. The program in the 1960s was to locate existing structures throughout the country which had heavy walls and roofs (or the intermediate stories of tall buildings)--in short, any space which one might occupy and be shielded from the penetrating gamma radiation emanating from radioactive particles outside. Basements were particularly attractive options since only the overhead slab was a possible source of penetrating radiation.

Civil Defense officials (along with their survey to locate existing high-quality space) enlisted the aid of architects and engineers in many universities to develop fallout slanting concepts which would encourage owners of new buildings to consider the incorporation of fallout protection into their designs. Many designs were developed, and it was found that in most cases the protection could be achieved without additional cost to the building. Subsequently, fallout protection was actually incorporated into many public and private buildings.

By the 1970s, a widely-held consensus had developed that something as complicated and terrible as nuclear war would likely be preceded by a period of intensifying crisis, and that properly developed plans could insure that most people could be moved out of the higher risk areas--those near military targets or those with substantial industrial capacity. The latter would include most of our medium to large cities.

Thus, the fallout slanting option appeared to be more reasonable for those less densely populated areas to which people would be moved, and the blast (direct effects) option for those buildings in the high risk areas. Not all people could be evacuated from the higher risk areas since some essential industries must continue as long as possible.

These two options still appear to be eminently feasible and reasonable. There is presently not enough good existing fallout shelter in buildings in those areas which must receive evacuees. The fallout protection would have to be provided by upgrading existing buildings. This procedure has been shown to be feasible but requires very good planning and a great deal of work during a crisis. Designs incorporating slanting fallout protection into new buildings in low risk areas are good national security.

The high-risk areas present a more difficult problem. Blast slanting cannot be done with "little or no additional cost," although it *can* be done with only a modest additional cost, however, which we cannot expect the building owner to assume. Present estimates indicate that blast protection can be incorporated into basements at an added cost of less than ten dollars per square foot of basement space. Basically, blast protection requires strengthening the slab over the basement, providing blast closures on entryways, and selecting buildings and sites which present the least mass fire threat.

In the light of risk area needs, studies were undertaken to develop design guidance which would permit blast effects protection to be incorporated into the basements of those buildings to be built in the higher risk areas. That guidance is currently available in the form of a design manual.

An obvious conclusion to be drawn from the above facts is that a new effort should be undertaken to encourage fallout slanting in low risk areas, and that some form of government subsidy should be provided to encourage blast slanting in high risk areas where such activities as food processing and handling must continue as long as possible to make an evacuation plan work. These measures are reasonable and deserve the support of everyone who is interested in our survival as a nation.

In the event of a nuclear attack on this country, do you believe that the general availability of potassium iodide and plans to use it would provide a practical measure for reducing the effects on the survivors of consuming food or water containing radioactive iodine?
(Respondent: Paul Skierkowski)

It is generally agreed that potassium iodide ("KI") is an effective agent that can block thyroid uptake of radioiodine due to ingestion or inhalation. However, the practicability and feasibility of using it as a thyroid protecting agent subsequent to a nuclear attack is, at best, questionable.

When considering the differences between radioiodine exposure from a nuclear attack and a nuclear (i.e. reactor) accident, terms such as Protective Action Guidance (PAG), Maximum Permissible Concentration (MPC) and Projected Dose Commitment are meaningless. And, although radioiodine will be a major fission fragment in the biosphere from any nuclear weapon usage, weapons source radioiodine is not identical to reactor source iodine. For example, in a reactor, ^{131}I will be the major radioiodine, whereas ^{132}I is the major source of exposure from weapons fission fragments. The dose per μCi for ^{132}I is 2 orders of magnitude less than that for ^{131}I.

What should be addressed and answered, therefore, is the ability of this action to meet the five "characteristics for good protective actions" (Shleien, 1983).

A protective action should be *effective*: it should substantially reduce population exposures below those that would otherwise occur. The use of potassium iodide as a thyroid blocking agent has been shown to meet this criterion when *used correctly* and *in the correct amount*. It should be noted that potassium iodide serves only as a thyroid protectant, and has no other organ protecting action against radiation effects; also, it is not effective against external radiation exposure to the thyroid.

A protective action should be *safe*: it must not introduce new health risks with potential consequences worse than the original problem. On an acute basis, there is enough incidence of adverse reaction to potassium iodide to question that these adverse reactions might not balance, or possibly exceed, the chronic effect of not using it, i.e., the *possibility* of thyroid carcinoma. Note that the possibility of adverse effects of using the potassium iodide when not indicated or in excessive amounts are not included in this analysis. If included, the balance would surely tip to the unsafe side.

A protective action should be *practical*: the logistics must be well developed at a reasonable cost and all legal problems solved. Providing potassium iodide to all *potential* survivors of an initial nuclear attack would mean prior distribution to the over 220 million citizens of the country, a formidable task in itself. As to cost, the initial cost of production plus distribution is not the final cost. The stability of the dosage form is such that new supplies would need to be distributed at approximately three-year intervals, as well as collection of old supplies to avoid many problems. At a conservative estimate of $.40 per individual dose package, this is a national expenditure of approximately $100 million every three years. (Note that at least one commercial firm has already jumped on this and offers a patient package for $10 plus $2 postage and handling.) The cost of production would probably be minor compared to the cost and work involved in development of a distribution system. The legal problems involved with misuse, e.g., the unnecessary ingestion and possible adverse reactions, has not been addressed by any agency.

A protective action should be *well defined* in terms of responsibility and authority for application: there must be no indecision due to jurisdictional misunderstanding between health and other agencies concerned with radiation control. This one should be easy to meet, assuming that agency is functional and can issue appropriate instructions *to the people affected* (not necessarily all the population).

A protective action should consider the possible *impact of the countermeasure* on the public, industry, agriculture, and government. When considering all the other medical, social, logistical and political implications of nuclear attack, it is doubtful that failure to provide this specific "protective action" will have a highly significant implication.

In summary, the efficacy of potassium iodide in protecting the thyroid from ingestion of radioiodine is not questioned. However, the cost and effort involved in providing for such a protective action plus other unanswered safety and legal questions are of such a magnitude as to make its use impractical, if not impossible.

What is the neutron bomb? How is it to be used? Should the civilian population be concerned about its effects? *(Respondent: Kenneth W. Skrable)*

The neutron bomb or enhanced nuclear warhead has been touted by the popular media as a new nuclear weapon that kills people without damaging buildings and property. It is proposed that the neutron bomb be used as a tactical weapon. It is not proposed as a strategic nuclear weapon as exemplified by the large scale thermonuclear devices carried by intercontinental ballistic missiles. In fact, the neutron bomb is proposed to be used to stop invading enemy forces without the collateral damage and death to persons outside the area of tactical application that normally occurs from thermal radiation and blast from currently stockpiled fission-based tactical weapons.

In the neutron bomb, the major portion of the energy released occurs by the fusion reaction, and most of this energy is associated with penetrating fast neutrons. It is a miniature hydrogen bomb. Most of the fast neutrons escape from the site of the detonation and create a neutron fluence, even inside the tanks of invading enemy troops, that causes radiation doses in excess of 10,000 rads,

enough to cause immediate incapacitation. The kinetic energy associated with the recoiling, non-penetrating helium nuclei that are produced in the fusion reaction does get degraded ultimately to heat, which leads to some blast and thermal radiation. However, because this part of the total energy released is relatively small, the lethality range associated with the neutron radiation exceeds that from blast and thermal radiation. This is not the case for tactical weapons whose energy yield is based upon the fission reaction. The lethality range of blast and thermal radiation from a fission tactical weapon exceeds that from the prompt neutrons and gamma rays released at the time of detonation.

Currently, stockpiled fission tactical weapons and the neutron bomb are in the energy yield of one to tens of kilotons of TNT equivalent. When a neutron bomb is exploded sufficiently above the surface of the earth, it could cause neutron doses in excess of 10,000 rads out to distances of several hundred yards without any significant blast or thermal radiation damage to the surrounding civilian population. Because of the rapid reduction of the neutron fluence by the inverse square law and attenuation, the neutron dose is reduced below the lethality range at relatively small distances outside the area of tactical usefulness. Tactical weapons whose energy yield is based upon the fission reaction, however, would cause considerable damage and death to the civilian population outside the area of tactical usefulness.

To understand why the tactical weapon creates more blast and thermal radiation, consider the specific fusion and fission reactions:

Fusion

$$^{2}_{1}H + ^{3}_{1}H \longrightarrow ^{*5}_{2}He \longrightarrow ^{4}_{2}He + ^{1}_{0}n + Q,$$

where Q = energy released = 17.6 MeV. In this fusion reaction, the neutron carries away 80% or 14.1 MeV of the energy released while the recoiling, non-penetrating He atom has a kinetic energy of 3.52 MeV that is locally absorbed and degraded to heat. This heat leads to minimal blast and thermal radiation.

Fission

$$^{239}_{94}Pu + ^{1}_{0}n \longrightarrow ^{*240}_{94}Pu$$
$$\longrightarrow ^{90}_{36}Kr + ^{146}_{58}Ce + 4^{1}_{0}n\text{'s} + ^{0}_{0}\gamma\text{'s} + Q,$$

where Q = total prompt energy released = 175 MeV. *[Editor's Note: This is but one example out of the scores of different fission reactions which occur. DJS]* Of this total prompt energy released, the fission fragments have about 93 percent, or 163 MeV, of recoil kinetic energy that is locally absorbed and degraded to heat while the prompt neutrons and gamma rays have the remainder, or 12 MeV, of the total energy released. When the fission fragment recoil kinetic energy is degraded to heat, materials making up the bomb reach temperatures of millions of degrees and are vaporized into a very hot, expanding plasma. This ultimately leads to blast and thermal radiation whose lethality range exceeds that from the neutrons and gamma rays released at the time of the detonation.

By replacing fission tactical weapons with neutron weapons, the tactical objective of the weapon will be maintained without the collateral damage and death to civilians outside the area of usefulness. Therefore, the neutron bomb, in fact, may be considered to be a bomb that benefits people, civilian people.

In summary and in answer to the questions:

The neutron bomb is a miniature hydrogen bomb. It is to be used as a tactical weapon against invading enemy forces. The civilian population, if ever tactical nuclear weapons had to be employed, should favor the neutron bomb over currently stockpiled fission based tactical weapons.

If located in an area where large fires developed, would not a shelter that provided adequate protection against initial nuclear weapons' effects and fallout nevertheless be subject to severe oxygen depletion, resulting in the death of the occupants? *(Respondent: Richard D. Small)*

There have been numerous studies of urban mass fires that might result as a consequence of a nuclear explosion. Although incomplete, a growing appreciation of the intensity and extent of these fires, as well as an understanding of the urban environment, is evolving.

Many buildings in a typical urban area are vulnerable to immediate ignition by thermal radiation or blast disruption. As a result, a distribution of fires involving many thousands of structures develops. At first, not all structures are fully involved; the fire evolution is a dynamic process. Some fires burn out; others spread to uninvolved structures. For long periods, however, the overall fire appears to be spatially and temporally continuous. After several hours, the fire decays.

Both numerical simulations and theoretical analyses have shown that such fires generate high velocity fire winds. A typical large area (mass) fire can induce measurable winds from areas four to nine times larger than the fire area. The velocities increase as the fire area is approached. As a consequence, large quantities of ambient air are drawn into the burning city. Street networks channel the fresh air throughout the city, and the amount of air available is several times in excess of that required to support the fires. Although in enclosed locations, fires may deplete the available oxygen supply. For fires in the open, an excess of oxygen is available. This conclusion is consistent with the complete burning of all available combustibles reported for World War II mass fires. In an oxygen-depleted environment such results are rare.

Although protection against the thermal environment should be considered in an effective shelter design, for most areas it does not seem probable that shelter occupants would die from oxygen starvation. The exceptions, however, are notable.

Fires in heavily built-up areas will require greater amounts of oxygen than fires in residential areas characterized by relatively low building densities. Such built-up areas may not have sufficient oxygen supply--at least temporarily. Shelters located in urban centers or densely built-up areas may require some emergency air supply. Construction of shelters under open areas such as parks, parking lots, and even streets may alleviate this requirement. There is an important caveat to this projection. Should heavily built-up areas be subject to extensive blast damage, debris will bury many combustibles implying a much lower fire intensity, and hence a reduced oxygen requirement.

Our analyses have shown that the fire environment, although severe, is characterized by high velocity fire winds that draw more than sufficient oxygen into the burning area. While an emergency air supply may be a prudent precaution in some shelter locations, for most of the urban area, no such provisions are necessary.

Over the years the National Council on Radiation Protection and Measurements (NCRP) has taken the lead in assessing the hazards of ionizing radiation and providing advice on the safe handling and use of sources of such radiation. Could you explain what the NCRP has done and is doing in connection with the ionizing radiation hazard that would be created in a nuclear attack? *(Respondent: Lewis V. Spencer)*

A scientific committee designated SC 63 was established a few years ago by the NCRP to write and work in this subject area. (I have served as chairman of that committee since its inception.)

It has always been my understanding that NCRP's original impetus, even prior to establishment of its Charter, was the stimulation and summarizing of information and recommendations about radiation sources, detectors, and biological effects, with better protection as a goal. A focus on the many important processes and applications involving radiation sources early led to the concept of "permissible exposures." After a long history of study and modifications, this concept is still basic to industries utilizing radioactive materials.

But such a concept implies controllability and is not applicable to possible uncontrolled exposures. In 1974, after much study of the project, NCRP Report No. 42 was issued, which summarized a point of view towards possible exposures which might be controlled, in terms of a "Penalty" Table (NCRP, 1974. This table is reproduced in Jack Greene's response, above). This simple table listed possible medical care requirements and indicated conservative lethality percentages for whole body radiation exposures during stated time intervals. One must be aware that severe early consequences of large radiation exposures can be avoided if intensity can be reduced and time interval of exposure extended.

This same report summarized information about radiation sources and types of injury resulting from detonation of a nuclear device in a populated area. To date the Penalty Table has not been revised, and the general information given in NCRP Report No. 42 is still valid.

Recent concern about Three Mile Island circumstances, and even more about the enormous build-up of nuclear weapon stockpiles resulted in the formation of Scientific Committee 63, whose first task was the planning for an NCRP-sponsored symposium on "The Control of Exposure to the Public to Ionizing Radiation in the Event of Accident or Attack," held in 1981. Objectives of this symposium included "collection, analysis, development and dissemination" of up-to-date and accurate information on a wide variety of emergencies involving major radiation hazards, discussion of this information, and clarifying "roles and responsibilities" of different government agencies, state and local, as well as federal. The status as of 1981 of our knowledge of exposure consequences, measures for limiting exposures, dosimetry, and the state of public information and training were all the subject of professional papers and discussion which has been recorded in the proceedings of the symposium.

Participants in SC 63 view our country's readiness for appropriate response to a major, rapidly developing, broadly distributed radiation hazard as dangerously lacking in necessary instrumentation, available trained personnel with detailed planning, and general public knowledge about effects, protection, and measurement. This applies not only to early and intense radiation hazards, but also to later consequences. A report in preparation by SC 63 addresses these general problems in a manner which is intended to make the report usable with a minimum of intermediate interpretation, to citizens as well as officials and specialists.

Our country has tended to act on the assumption that the types of weaponry existing and under development would either not ever be used in our country, or would quickly kill everyone and render such problems as the above ignorable. But the real world has a very long future, is not as tidy as this myth would have us believe, and involves existing powerful nuclear devices, many pointed at targets in this country. Public knowledge of, and preparedness in detail for, possible disasters involving radiation hazards is a must, not one more option. The availability of up-to-date information in usable form is the related and reasonable NCRP objective, fully consistent with the NCRP Charter.

Would one expect to find a significantly higher-than-normal incidence of cancer (caused by radiation) among workers associated with nuclear weapons production and testing programs, given that this large group of people has been exposed to above-background radiation levels for a long time? *(Respondent: Daniel J. Strom)*

To answer this question, one needs to know the numbers of people involved, and the collective dose equivalents these people received on the job. Also needed are the average dose equivalent received, and the time since exposure (for cancer latency). These numbers can be used, along with the radiogenic cancer risk estimates of the National Academy of Sciences (the "BEIR III Report," NAS, 1980), the United Nations Scientific Committee on the Effects of Atomic Radiation (UNSCEAR, 1982), or the International Commission on Radiological Protection (ICRP, 1977) to make a "back-of-the-envelope" estimate of numbers of excess cancers caused by radiation. This approach is simplistic in the sense that it does not take into account the age distributions of the population, or the age at time of exposure, but it nonetheless serves as a useful rough estimate.

Numbers of Persons Exposed

U.S. personnel who have been occupationally exposed to radiation in the course of the development, production, and testing of nuclear weapons include civilians and military, and some who have been in both groups.

The U.S. Department of Energy (DOE) Health and Mortality Studies include some 500,000 persons (not all of whom have been exposed to radiation on the job) employed by DOE or predecessor agencies (ERDA, AEC, or the Manhattan Project) or their contractors, and about 100,000 persons employed at shipyards doing nuclear propulsion work on ships and submarines (Lushbaugh, 1982). The Defense Nuclear Agency's (DNA) Nuclear Test Personnel Review (NTPR) lists 250,000 persons involved in weapons testing, both military and civilian, including some already counted in the DOE Health and Mortality Studies (Defense Nuclear Agency, 1984). Assuming that 100,000 of the DNA people were civilians already counted in DOE's 500,000, this gives us a round total of about 750,000 people, counting the shipyard workers. As explained below, perhaps only one third, or *250,000 people*, received measurable exposures.

Collective Dose Equivalent

The average dose equivalent to the NTPR personnel (including the civilians) was about 0.5 rem. This gives a collective dose equivalent of about 125,000 person-rem. The collective dose equivalent to the shipyard workers is 153,558 person-rem for the period 1954 to 1979, averaging less than 3000 person-rem per year over the past few years. So, for 1954 to 1984, the collective dose at the shipyards is roughly 170,000 person-rem.

The collective dose equivalent at the other DOE facilities is much harder to gauge, because many of the data have not been published. At one national laboratory, from 1943 through 1978, the collective dose equivalent was less than 30,000 person-rem distributed among some 20,000 workers (Parrish, 1982), while at another weapons facility, the collective effective dose equivalent has been estimated as roughly 30,000 person-rem distributed among some 16,000 workers between 1950 and 1980 (Strom, 1984). Taking these two facilities as representative of the 400,000 DOE personnel not involved in weapons testing, one arrives at a collective dose somewhere between 600,000 and 800,000 person-rem.

This comes to a grand total of *under 1,000,000 person-rem* outside the shipyards, with another *170,000 person-rem* at the shipyards.

Average Dose Equivalent

NTPR lists the average dose equivalent as 0.5 rem for its personnel. At one of the shipyards, the average career dose equivalent was 2.8 rem among those exposed (one-third of all workers), or less than one rem averaged over the entire population. The average career dose equivalent at DOE may be in the range of 1 to 2 rem. It must be pointed out, however, that many (two-thirds at one shipyard for which data are available) workers have never received any measurable exposure. Assuming that only one-third of the 650,000 non-shipyard workers ever received any exposure, one computes average career dose equivalents of 1,000,000 rem/217,000 persons = *5 rem* for DOE and 170,000 rem/33,000 people = *5 rem* for the shipyards *among those actually exposed*. The only point of this calculation is that these exposures are, on the average, clearly *low doses* of radiation for which the risk estimates below are assumed to be valid.

It is also interesting to point out that, for a 50-year old person receiving 0.1 rem each year from natural background, these average career doses are roughly equal to the cumulative natural background doses.

Time Since Exposure

Current models invoke a two- to ten-year interval following exposure for risk of leukemia, and a 10- to 40-year interval following exposure for risk of solid tumors. Turning this around, one would expect to have seen all leukemias resulting from exposures prior to 1974, and considerably less than all solid tumors resulting from exposures after 1944. The point is that not all cancers caused by exposures to date have actually appeared yet. For exposures since 1974, essentially no solid tumors have appeared under this model. Without knowing how many persons of which ages were exposed to what doses in which years, a better answer is not available. For this calculation, let us assume that only *one-half* of the total number of radiogenic cancers that will appear (due to exposures prior to 1984) have already appeared.

Expected Numbers of Cancers

The risk estimates for low doses are summarized in Table G. All estimates are probably overestimates (as discussed in the source documents) at the levels of exposure in these populations; specifically, the BEIR III estimates are for higher doses (10 rads acute or 70 rads at 1 rad/year), and one is told that they are not valid at lower doses.

Table G. Radiation Risk Coefficients (Fatal Cancers per Million Person-Rems).

BEIR I (1972)	50-165 (27 years)
ICRP # 26 (1977)	100
UNSCEAR (1977, 1982)	75-175
BEIR III (1980)	67-226 (variety of models)

Using the BEIR III numbers, which bracket the others, for 1,000,000 person-rem one expects 67 to 226 excess cancers, and for 170,000 person-rem one expects 11 to 38 excess cancers. Using the BEIR III spontaneous fatal cancer rate of 164,000 per million, one calculates the expected cancer rates in these populations, as shown in Table H.

Table H. Expected Cancer Rates in U.S. Worker Populations.

	Number 1000s	1000 person-rem	natural cancers	radiogenic cancers	% excess
DOE+NTPR	217	1000	35600	67-226	.2-.6
SHIPYARDS	33	170	5400	11-38	.2-.7
TOTALS	250	1170	41000	78-264	.2-.7

Since cancer is a randomly occurring disease in the absence of radiation exposure, it is unlikely that excess cancer deaths of the order of 0.2 percent to 0.7 percent could be discerned at a convincing level of statistical significance in a population of this size. Certainly the excess cancers would not appear to be an epidemic. It is important to note that one expects only half of the radiogenic cancers to have occurred; but not all spontaneous cancers have occurred, either, so the percentages may not be that far off.

With refinements in the calculations, and more accurate numbers and doses, it can be shown that epidemiologic studies may be able to detect rare cancers among highly-exposed subgroups of these populations at a convincing level of statistical significance, if the above risk estimates are correct.

What genetic effects resulting from ionizing radiation exposures could be expected among the survivors of a nuclear attack? *(Respondent: Daniel J. Strom)*

The genetic effects of exposure to ionizing radiation are changes that occur in germ cells of parents due to exposure to radiation *before* conception. (Radiation effects occurring between conception and birth are called teratogenic effects.) Genetic effects, if they do not result in failure to conceive, failure to implant, or pre-natal death, may be passed on to future generations.

Radiation-induced transmitted genetic effects have not been seen at statistically significant levels in human populations although there is a suggestion of genetic effects in the Japanese bomb survivors. The evidence of radiation-induced genetic effects in animals, however, is so strong that there can be little doubt about genetic effects in human beings.

A reason for the lack of statistically significant human data is the large incidence of genetic effects that occurs naturally--that is, from causes other than radiation exposures. According to the *BEIR III Report*, "more than one percent of all children born will have a simply-inherited disease causing an appreciable handicap" (NAS, 1980). Elsewhere in the report is the statement "the current incidence ... of human genetic disorder is approximately 107,000 cases per million liveborn." The majority of this 10.7 percent incidence rate, perhaps 90 percent of it, however, does not result in appreciable handicaps.

Current risk estimates from BEIR III are 5 to 75 serious genetic disorders per million liveborn offspring per rad in the first generation. For example, if each average non-sterile parent surviving a nuclear war received 100 *genetically significant* rads, the risk estimate would be

(100 rad/parent)(2 parents/child)(5 to 75×10^{-6}/rad)

= 1,000 to 15,000 serious genetic disorders per million liveborn in the first generation of the survivors offspring--a rate of 0.1 percent to 1.5 percent. This would be in the range of "much less than" to "about equal to" the current naturally occurring rate of serious genetic disorders which according to a BEIR III assumption is "more than one percent."

Parents receiving higher or lower doses would, presumably, have proportionately higher or lower risks. A dose of 200 rads to each parent would double the above calculated percentages to 0.2 percent to 3 percent. There is a practical upper limit to the genetic damage that would be passed on to a future generation. Most people receiving doses above about five hundred rads during the first week or so would not survive, and therefore would not procreate or contribute damage to the gene pool. Further, those who survive the high radiation doses might be subject to temporary or permanent sterility (Mettler, Jr., and Moseley, Jr., 1985).

Another way of viewing genetic risks is to use the "doubling dose" concept. The doubling dose has been estimated at about 150 rads in the Japanese survivors (Schull, Otake, and Neel, 1981). Applying this approach results in about the same numbers as the higher end of the BEIR III method as used above.

What is the basis for believing that Civil Defense measures could have any effect on the consequences of a nuclear attack, and is there a research base from which a reliable answer to this question can be drawn? *(Respondent: Walmer Strope)*

The advent of nuclear weapons immediately ended the historical practice of preparing to fight the last war better the next time. Although the vulnerability of the civilian society and war economy to direct attack was demonstrated in World War II, nuclear weapons created a new dimension, especially in regard to Civil Defense. The Federal Civil Defense Administration (FCDA), established in 1950, was soon actively engaged in research and development activities. Most of this research concentrated on understanding weapon effects and developing the basis for the central countermeasures, shelter and evacuation.

Participation at the nuclear weapons tests of the 1950s was continuous and done in cooperation with the Civil Effects Test Group of the Atomic Energy Commission. Early emphasis was on the cost and feasibility of blast shelter for high risk areas. Effort also was pushed on fallout modeling and decontamination. A number of evacuation experiments were conducted, such as that in which the downtown area of Portland, Oregon, was emptied. In 1956, a computerized damage assessment system was developed by FCDA that permitted analysis of a nationwide nuclear attack. The early studies demonstrated that relatively modest fallout protection factors could be effective in preventing fatalities from fallout radiation. A goal of a protection factor (PF) of 1000 had been set on the basis of "worst case" studies. The nationwide assessments showed that most of the population was not in the worst case situation and that PFs of 100, or even 40, would make a substantial difference. Experimental surveys of buildings in several counties scattered across the country found much of this kind of shelter. These data, together with the fact that Congress had failed to fund a blast shelter building program during the 1950s, led to the fallout shelter program of the Kennedy administration.

Radiation from fallout was a persistent hazard, even though the threat diminished with time through radioactive decay and physical weathering of the fallout particles themselves. People would need to remain sheltered for an extended period of time, a period measured in terms of weeks, not days, in most instances. Two weeks shelter stay was a planning figure adopted on the basis of the slowing of decay and the estimated time needed to organize remedial movement operations. An early question was whether effete Americans would tolerate weeks cooped up in crowded shelters. The first experiments addressed this question. Space allotments were generous (20 to 40 square feet per person) and bunks, furniture, and traditional foods were provided. It was found that volunteers tolerated confinement well. By the mid-1960s, over 5,000 men, women, and children, from babes in arms to octogenarians, had participated in shelter occupancy experiments, which had as their main objective finding out how austere the shelter environment could be. People tolerated sleeping on the floor, space allotments as little as six square feet per person (10 square feet per person became the standard), and eating wheat-based shelter crackers.

Water and ventilation were the keys to prolonged shelter occupancy. These were interconnected issues. When people were crowded together, their body heat created a hot, sweaty atmosphere that increased water demand. If drinking water were available in unlimited quantities, a hot, humid environment could be tolerated. If water is limited, ventilation must be increased to control temperature and humidity. The likely loss of electrical power rules out air conditioning and running water. Methods of water storage and handpowered ventilation, together with the physiological and psychological studies needed to evaluate standards, became an important area of Civil Defense research in the 1960s.

Appropriations for Civil Defense during the early 1950s averaged about $60 million annually, equivalent in buying power to the annual appropriation of today. During the 1950s, a large number of technical manuals and bulletins were issued that reflected both the operational concerns and the research and developmental basis for guidance and training. Leadership in shelters was one of the operational concerns that was addressed in the shelter occupancy tests of the early 1960s. Training programs for shelter managers emerged from this work. Training of radiological monitors and Radiological Defense Officers also was stressed. The Soviet detonation of a thermo-nuclear device in 1954, together with our own experience with the Marshallese natives, led to extensive development of radiation-detecting instrumentation. The instruments developed for FCDA and Office of Civil and Defense Mobilization (OCDM) were the best of their day and became the basis for a major procurement. Maintenance and calibration of these same instruments is still a major field operation today.

The Civil Defense research effort has exerted leadership in the free world in a number of subject areas, including fire effects and countermeasures, evacuation, and post-attack recovery. Each of these areas deserves a summary note.

The fire consequences of nuclear attack have been a major source of uncertainty with respect to survival estimates, the design of shelters against air blast and other direct effects, and the proposed use of "best available shelter," such as building basements, where specially constructed shelters are not provided. The firestorms of World War II bombings of German cities received wide publicity. Firestorms were presumed to be the natural consequence of nuclear attack. However, the detonations at Hiroshima and Nagasaki did not create the expected phenomena, and the resulting fatalities and injuries could be accounted for without considering fire as a causative factor. Indeed, some evidence was found that suggested that flames ignited by the heat flash from the detonation were snuffed out by the blast wave that followed. Weapons tests were never held under conditions that allowed direct experimentation on mass fires. Operation Flambeau used a multitude of piles of forest slash to model fire growth and spread, and to assess the atmospheric circulation produced by a mass fire. Fires were created over buried shelters and measurements made in basements as buildings were put to the torch. A blast facility was built in which whole rooms could be exposed to megaton-scale overpressures. Experiments in this facility soon demonstrated that fire ignitions could be extinguished by modest blast overpressures. Despite these advances in knowledge, the fire consequences of nuclear attack are still uncertain and, indeed, controversial. Most recently, smoke and soot assumed to be produced by nuclear fires have been alleged to be capable of modifying the climate for a considerable period of time.

Evacuation of hazard areas and areas at risk has always been a central Civil Defense countermeasure. In the 1950s, the failure to obtain a shelter construction program led to the adoption of evacuation planning as the main lifesaving concept of the pre-fallout era. Whole cities were to be evacuated in a matter of hours upon detection of propeller-driven bombers in

Table I. Civil Defense Research Obligations, 1962-1971.

Research Areas and Projects	Ten-Year Costs
SHELTER RESEARCH	$28,682,094
Protection Studies	10,229,449
Shelter Environment Studies	4,442,068
Subsistence & Habitability Studies	1,758,393
Prototype Life Support Systems	1,769,666
Shelter Management Studies	3,471,378
Shelter Systems Studies	3,206,646
Development & Test	3,804,494
SUPPORT SYSTEMS RESEARCH	20,217,292
Monitoring Systems Studies	2,447,833
Communications & Warning Studies	3,394,249
Reduction of Vulnerability	1,294,647
Emergency Medical Studies	2,521,184
Fire Effects & Protection	8,059,054
Emergency Operations Research	2,500,325
POST-ATTACK RESEARCH	16,169,570
Radiological Phenomena & Effects	4,635,224
Radiological Countermeasures	4,202,329
Repair & Reclamation	2,481,537
PA Medical, Health, Welfare Studies	1,612,234
Post-attack Systems Studies	3,238,246
SYSTEMS EVALUATION	21,035,001
Civil Defense System Analysis	7,606,379
Strategic Analyses	1,341,220
Vulnerability Studies	3,043,327
Organization & Training Studies	1,373,455
Planning Support Research	1,572,185
Information Systems Studies	1,086,041
Physical Environment Studies	1,405,000
Social & Psychological Studies	3,607,394
TOTAL	$86,103,957

flight over the North Pole. A considerable amount of research was the basis for this planning. With the advent of ballistic missiles, the time available for evacuation was seen to be too short. Throughout the 1960s, however, research continued on the use of evacuation in a crisis period. Since several days would be available for movement of people from the cities to the countryside, the means to house and feed them and to provide them with fallout shelter in the event of attack were found to be a more critical problem than the actual exodus. Also in question was whether any President would encounter circumstances that would cause him or her to order the cities evacuated even if the capability existed. Thus, crisis relocation, as it was later called, remained a research topic until it was discovered in the late 1960s that city evacuation was a central element in Soviet Civil Defense.

The definition of Civil Defense in the applicable law confines it to life-saving and immediate, if temporary, repairs to damaged facilities. Nonetheless, research on post-attack conditions and recovery therefrom has been an important component of Civil Defense research from the beginning, and especially during the 1960s and 1970s. In part, this emphasis resulted because both Presidents and Congresses have insisted upon knowing what the longer-term consequences of investments in immediate life-saving would be. And, of course, end-of-mankind predictions have been the last resort of the opponents of Civil Defense when efforts to deride particular programs have failed. As shown in Table I, about $16 million of research funds were expended on post-attack research during the 1960s. About one-half of the effort was devoted to the study of fallout phenomena and countermeasures. A major effort was made to conceptualize the recovery process and to invent systems and organizations to accomplish it. This work currently is the primary basis for government planning in this field.

Because Civil Defense is an activity to prepare for surviving a nuclear attack--attack for which there is no historical analog--strategic studies that attempt to organize what we know about this future contingency and to assess the outcome given various assumed preparations always have been an important subject area for research. The 1956 damage assessment system was one of the earliest products of this type. Because funding for Civil Defense has always been limited, cost-effectiveness analyses as a guide to budget preparation and justification have enjoyed considerable support. In an attempt to understand more fully the state of knowledge in the complex and arcane field of Civil Defense, one mechanism adopted was the "Five City Study," in which all of the researchers under contract to the Office of Civil Defense were made to apply their expertise to the brick-by-brick analysis of a series of nuclear attack scenarios. From this effort came numerous results, insights, and priorities for further study.

In the event of a nuclear war, would the expected increase in the sun's ultraviolet radiation reaching the earth's surface, due to the weakening of the ozone layer, preclude the continued survival and recovery of those people fortunate enough to have been spared from the other effects of the attack? Further, is it reasonable to fear that this enhanced radiation would seriously threaten other, if not all, forms of life on the planet? *(Respondent: Edward Teller)*

I do not believe so. My conclusion is that the problems related to a weakening of the ozone layer seem manageable, and with the rapid elimination of weapons large enough to cause ozone layer damage, the probability of serious ozone layer depletion is dropping significantly.

In the 1970s, concern arose about the possible effects of a nuclear conflict on the ozone layer (National Academy of Sciences, 1975; MacCracken and Chang, 1975). The small amounts of ozone present in the stratosphere play an important role in shielding the earth from ultraviolet radiation. Large nuclear explosions propel the contents of their fireballs, including the molecules NO and NO_2 (these oxides are collectively referred to as NO_x), into the high atmosphere where these molecules effectively would react with ozone, eventually converting ozone to oxygen molecules (O_2).

If injected in sufficient quantity at high altitude, the NO_x could deplete the ozone layer significantly. The ozone molecules are steadily regenerated by solar radiation, but the presence of the NO_x residue from large nuclear explosions could reduce the effective thickness of the ozone layer by an average of 30 to 40 percent from its usual level for a period of a year or two (Chang et al., 1979; Luther, 1983). (For purposes of comparison, the effective thickness of the ozone layer during summer is about 20 percent less over Miami than over Seattle.) Complete recovery would take several more years (Luther, 1983).

Assuming the explosion of thousands of megaton-yield weapons, the calculated diminution of the ozone layer would give rise to increased serious sunburn immediately and to an increased incidence of skin cancer over an extended time. These primary effects, like the possibility of eye damage, could be countered with simple precautions. A secondary concern is that ozone depletion and consequent increase in ultraviolet radiation would destroy ultraviolet-sensitive plants or plankton species, and would harm early springtime plant growth, with important effects on ecosystem viability (Caldwell, 1979).

Since, in the middle latitudes, observed natural variations of the ozone column are comparable to the predicted effects following a nuclear war using megaton weapons, the changes are not apt to be highly significant (Office of Technology Assessment, 1979). However, the most pertinent consideration is that the present U.S. arsenal has few nuclear explosives with the great yield that is a necessary precondition for depletion of the ozone layer. The same trend toward smaller, more accurately aimed, and less costly weapons also has been adopted, with some delay, by the Soviet Union.

Considering the advancements in micro-electronics and in radiation sensors, how long will it be before a very inexpensive "wrist-watch" size radiation measuring device that measures all types of ionizing radiation and covers the range from background to hundreds of R per hour becomes available? *(Respondent: C. John Umbarger)*

Over the past several years, significant advances have been made by the commercial electronics industry in developing low power (CMOS) tiny microprocessors. Accompanying recent advances in low power and sensitive tiny radiation detectors and associated electronics now make possible the production of very small, yet "smart," radiation monitoring instruments that should weigh no more than one to two ounces, including batteries and displays. With custom or semi-custom hybrid or integrated circuits, instrument packages can approach standard film badge or even wrist-watch sizes. Properly designed and calibrated, such tiny devices would be very useful in personnel radiation exposure and dosimetry monitoring and recording. The small size makes the monitor convenient to carry (or wear) throughout the workplace, hence increasing worker acceptance and use and, therefore, significantly improving worker protection. The "smart" aspect allows easy tailoring of device features (functions, calibrations, alarms, etc.) to user requirements.

Tiny solid state detectors, either HgI or CdTe, and miniature GM tubes have been utilized in small radiation warning devices, "chirpers", that have a total weight of approximately one ounce, and will operate for many months on one or two batteries under normal use. The small monitors are appropriate for general beta/gamma detection, with some application for other types of radiation monitoring.

Recently, Los Alamos coupled a microprocessor chip with their earlier tiny chirper design to demonstrate the feasibility of building small, active, radiation monitors and dosimeters using current technology. The actual CdTe detector hybrid is close to being watch-sized. While much work must be performed to develop tiny detectors with optimum characteristics, especially relating to radiation energy dependence and, possibly, radiation damage effects, it seems quite reasonable that commercial grade smart, active and miniature radiation monitors should be available in quantity by 1987 or 1988 at the latest.

How practical is it to design and build a Civil Defense shelter that would protect its occupants from the heat and noxious gases that could be created by the mass fires that could rage overhead? *(Respondent: T. E. Waterman)*

Civil Defense shelters can be built to withstand both conducted heat and resist the penetration of hot and noxious gases. The secrets of success are to assure a complete shelter envelope and to judiciously select the locations of shelter air intakes. A building basement, even if covered by a substantial ceiling, is not automatically a good shelter. Voids such as plumbing and electrical chases from above must be sealed so that they resist flow of combustion products to the shelter space.

Large scale experiments have shown that a twelve-inch concrete ceiling limits shelter heating by an overhead residential debris fire to amounts similar to that generated by the shelter occupants. These same experiments demonstrated that early application of one-third gallon of water per square foot of floor area over the shelter reduces heat loading to 25 percent of that otherwise encountered.

Also, it was shown that while attempting to pull ventilating air through a debris pile quickly filled the shelter with lethal levels of carbon monoxide, clearing a 15-foot diameter area around the air intake reduced CO in the shelter to tolerable levels. Thus, several intakes and a CO detector to assist in selecting which to use is a viable solution. Obviously, there will be congested building areas not suitable for locating shelters as debris will blanket the area if within the heavily blast-damaged zone.

Further experiments have shown that blast cracking of the shelter ceiling can be successfully countered by mechanically ventilating the shelter space to produce a slightly positive pressure. Water sprays directed into the cracks are not effective since hot water and additional debris will fall back into the shelter. Wet cloths make effective patches to block the fall of burning embers and reduce the ventilation air requirements for pressurization. Low melting point metals (electronics assemblies, etc.) are a particular problem if they are in the overall debris.

A buried shelter suffers none of the above heating problems and, properly located and vented, can limit the intake of hot and noxious gases. Our experiments did not address possible air contamination of the entire region from mass fire effects. It is expected that this problem can be addressed by others. Certainly, regions away from the center of mass fires will experience respirable air (Waterman, 1970; Takata and Waterman, 1972; Waterman, 1973; Waterman, 1974).

Considering the advancements in micro-electronics and in radiation sensors, how long will it be before a very inexpensive "wrist-watch" size radiation measuring device that measures all types of ionizing radiation and covers the range from background to hundreds of R per hour becomes available? *(Respondent: H.N. Wilson)*

Of course no one knows the precise answer, but an engineering "best guess" can be made. The military and Civil Defense are interested in such a device and development efforts are in progress. The desire is to have an instrument that will monitor both dose rate and dose from background to hundredths of rad/h. The initial design will probably be for gamma rays only.

We are all familiar with the digital watch with alarm features and some that play tunes. Some also include a small calculator. It seems evident that the digital circuitry and display technology exists at a high level of development. To produce the digital and display portion of an instrument is essentially just a problem of time and money.

The real problem is similar to the one recently experienced by the automotive industry in the use of microprocessors, which is the initial sensor and the accompanying signal conditioning electronics. For our case, the sensor is a gamma ray detector and by necessity it must be physically small, rugged, relatively immune to radiation damage, and of course, inexpensive. The solid state detector appears attractive for the job, but there are many problems involved. Most detectors require a bias voltage, and it is usually high compared to the instrument battery voltage. Also, if used in the normal pulse mode, a high gain, wide bandwidth, low-noise amplifier is required. Additional modes of operation may also be utilized. These and other signal conditioning tasks must be accomplished with a very low power consumption and still meet the wide dynamic range requirements. Such a detector and front end electronics package does not exist but must be developed. Work is in progress to develop and design such an instrument, but this may easily require two or three years of elapsed time. Once the basic design is complete, it must be reduced to the level of one or two silicon chips and then be incorporated in an appropriate package. This stage may easily require two or more years. Thus, in an attempt to answer the original question, an optimistic response would be at least four years, and a more realistic number is probably eight or ten. The cost of chip development and design could easily be $250 thousand to $500 thousand. To meet the requirement of being inexpensive, the instrument would need to be produced in very large quantities. This, in turn, would occur only if there is a general acceptance and desire by the public for such an instrument.

BIOGRAPHICAL SKETCHES

Lee T. Battes
Director, Radiological Intelligence Services
Division of Military and Naval Affairs
State of New York
Public Security Building
State Campus
Albany, NY 12226

Mr. Battes is currently the Director of the Technical Resources Section of the New York State Emergency Management Office (SEMO). In 1974 he joined the Radiological Intelligence Section of the New York State Office of Disaster Preparedness (now SEMO) and became its Director in 1980. He has been involved with radiological protection aspects of disaster preparedness, including statewide management of Civil Defense instrumentation, planning assistance, training programs and emergency operations. His technical specialties include effects of nuclear war, off-site response for nuclear power plant accidents, and emergency response to radioactive transportation accidents.

Mr. Battes received a B.S. in Physics from Case Institute of Technology and an M.S. in Physics from the State University of New York. Additional health physics training was acquired at the University of Lowell, Massachusetts, and at the Nevada Test Site.

John W. Billheimer, Ph.D.
SYSTAN, INC.
343 Second Street
P.O. Box U
Los Altos, CA 94022

Dr. Billheimer is Vice President of SYSTAN, Inc., a consulting firm. He has more than twenty years of experience in investigating problems of food distribution and transportation under emergency conditions. As a consultant for FEMA and its predecessor agencies, he traced existing food distribution patterns, studied the vulnerability of the national food and transportation system to nuclear attack, conducted transportation industry workshops, investigated the feasibility of large-scale evacuations, and developed evacuating planning guidelines. In addition to his food and transportation studies for FEMA, Dr. Billheimer has led a variety of research studies for a wide range of clients, including the United States Department of Transportation (DOT), the California Department of Transportation, the California Highway Patrol, and private industrial clients. He recently completed an *Evaluation Handbook* designed to assist DOT planners, managers, and contractors in evaluating the impacts of transportation projects. Dr. Billheimer's work in evaluating the controversial diamond land project on the Santa Monica Freeway in Los Angeles was awarded the outstanding transportation planning study published in 1979 by the National Academy of Science Transportation Research Board.

Dr. Billheimer received a B.S. in Electrical Engineering from the University of Detroit (1961), an M.S. in E.E. from Massachusetts Institute of Technology (1963), and a Ph.D. in Industrial Engineering from Stanford University (1971).

Edward T. Bramlitt, Ph.D.
8813 Osito N.E.
Albuquerque, NM 87111

Dr. Bramlitt has been with Field Command, Defense Nuclear Agency, for ten years as Health Physicist responsible for planning the radiological clean-up of Enewetak Atoll, developing plans and procedures for responding to nuclear weapon accidents, managing radiation safety for FCDNA personnel involved in underground nuclear weapon tests, nuclear weapon inspections, and maintaining a readiness to test capability at Johnston Atoll. He spent seven years with Atomics International in reactor development and for space applications, as well as five years with the United States Navy, where he was assigned to the Office of Civil Defense and Defense Civil Preparedness Agency in an advisory capacity in nuclear engineering and related areas. He perfected criteria for the DCPA Standard Method of radiation shielding analysis, and served on a National Academy of Sciences Subcommittee with the task of characterizing the initial nuclear radiation environment and critical parameters for INR protection. Dr. Bramlitt is a Qualified Instructor in shelter analysis, and has taught protective construction at the Navy Civil Engineering Corps Officers School and DCPA Summer Institutes. He developed radiation safety plans and a radioactive plutonium simulant for large-scale nuclear weapon accident exercises; he also served as Radiological Safety Officer for Nuclear Weapon Accident Exercises (NUWAX) in 1979, 1981, and 1983. His current efforts include managing a radiological clean-up of alpha emitters in the environment at Johnston Atoll.

His academic research dealt with high-energy neutron interactions, and Dr. Bramlitt received his

Ph.D. in Nuclear Chemistry from the University of Arkansas.

Charles J. Bridgman, Ph.D.
Professor of Nuclear Engineering
Department of Engineering Physics
Air Force Institute of Technology
Wright-Patterson Air Force Base
Dayton, OH 28705

Dr. Bridgman is currently Professor and Chairman of the Nuclear Engineering Committee at the Air Force Institute. He teaches graduate courses in nuclear effects, and his research interests include radiation transport and nuclear effects, particularly fallout.

He received his B.S. from the United States Naval Academy (1952) and his Ph.D. in Nuclear Engineering from North Carolina State University (1963).

Conrad Chester, Ph.D.
Energy Division
Oak Ridge National Laboratory
P.O. Box X
Oak Ridge, TN 37830

Dr. Chester is a member of the senior research staff of the Oak Ridge National Laboratory. He currently directs the Emergency Planning Group of Regional and Urban Studies Section of the Energy Division in work on earth-sheltered structures for FEMA, and response to radiological emergencies for FEMA and DOE. He has been conducting research in Civil Defense since 1965, when he joined the Oak Ridge Civil Defense Research project under the direction of Eugene Wigner. He has worked on a wide variety of problems, including expedient shelter, protection against biological weapons, and effects of nuclear weapons on nuclear reactors. He has been with the Oak Ridge National Laboratory for twenty-seven years.

Dr. Chester received a B.S. in Chemical Engineering from Cornell University, and an M.S. and Ph.D. in Chemical Engineering from the University of Tennessee.

Roger J. Cloutier
Oak Ridge Associated Universities
P.O. Box 117
Oak Ridge, TN 37830

Since 1957, Mr. Cloutier has directed the Professional Training activities of the Oak Ridge associated Universities' Manpower Education, Research and Training Division. This group provides short-term training for approximately 1,000 scientists and engineers, as well as training programs for college and university faculty and students. Mr. Cloutier is especially knowledgeable about the health effects of energy use and is interested in the development of methods for the safe use of radionuclides in medicine and industry. He is a member and past president of the Health Physics Society. Other professional organizations include the International Radiation Protection Association, the Society of Nuclear Medicine, the American Association of Physicists in Medicine, the Sigma XI Society, and the Tennessee Academy of Sciences.

Mr. Cloutier received a B.S. in Zoology-Physics from the University of Massachusetts (1956), and an M.S. in Radiation Biology from the University of Rochester (1957). He was certified in Health Physics by the American Board of Health Physics in 1963.

Martin O. Cohen, Ph.D.
Mathematical Applications Group, Inc. (MAGI)
3 Westchester Plaza
Elmsford, NY 10523

Dr. Cohen is currently the Corporate Research Projects Director of MAGI. He has been extensively involved in the development and application of computer software for studies of nuclear radiation and transport through the atmosphere and complex configurations. He has written over 100 technical publications, many of which involve the prediction of prompt and fallout radiation effects from both tactical and strategic nuclear weapons.

Dr. Cohen received his Ph.D. in Nuclear Science and Engineering from Columbia University (1965).

D. A. Crossley, Jr., Ph.D.
Professor of Entomology
University of Georgia
Athens, GA 30601

In 1956, D. A. Crossley ("Dac") joined the emerging ecology group in the Health Physics Division of the Oak Ridge National Laboratory, where he worked with ecological consequences of radioactive waste disposal. His research concerned the movement of radioactive materials along insect food chains and radiation effects on insects. In 1967, Dr. Crossley became a Professor of Entomology at the University of Georgia, and a member of the Institute of Ecology. He has participated in research on nutrient cycling in forested ecosystems (at Coweta Hydrologic Laboratory, North Carolina) and in agro-ecosystems. He is a member of the Steering

Committee for the National Science Foundation's Long-Term Ecological Research program. He is a former Chairman of the University of Georgia's Radiation Safety Committee and a member of the Executive Committee of the Institute of Ecology. Currently, he is Graduate Coordinator for Georgia's interdisciplinary Degree Program in Ecology.

Dr. Crossley received his B.A. (1949) and his M.S. (1951) degrees in Biology from Texas Tech University; he studied mite taxonomy and biology at the University of Kansas, where he received his Ph.D. in 1956.

Wayne L. Davis
Scientific Consultant
2211 Altura Ave, N. E.
Albuquerque, NM 87110

From 1952 to 1957, Mr. Davis was first a Staff Member and later a consultant in the Systems Analysis Department at Sandia Corporation. At Sandia, and later at Dikewood Corporation, he performed and directed numerous studies in his special field of nuclear weapons effects and phenomenology as they affect both personnel and complex military systems. Mr. Davis joined the Dikewood Corporation in 1975 and later became both President and Chairman of the Board. In 1982, Dikewood Corporation joined with Kaman Sciences Corporation (KSC), where Mr. Davis remained until 1983 as Vice President of KSC and General Manager of Dikewood. He is currently a private consultant. Mr. Davis is listed in *Who's Who in the West, Who's Who in Finance and Industry, Who's Who in Frontiers of Science and Technology, American Men and Women of Science*, and is a member of numerous honorary fraternal organizations.

Mr. Davis received a B.S. in Engineering Physics (1952) and an M.S. in Electrical Engineering (1959) from the University of New Mexico.

Philip J. Dolan
Lockheed Missiles & Space Co,.
1111 Lockheed Way
Sunnyvale, CA 94088-3504

Mr. Dolan has acquired more than thirty-seven years of experience in research areas dealing with nuclear weapons and their effects, beginning with an assignment to the Manhattan District at Los Alamos in 1948. Subsequent Army assignments included those in Armed Forces Special Weapons Project in Albuquerque, N.M. and Washington, D.C., and the Defense Atomic Support Agency in Washington, D.C.. (both of which were successor organizations to the Manhattan District and predecessors of the Defense Nuclear Agency); he was appointed as an instructor in Nuclear Weapons Employment at the Army Command and General Staff College, and as Nuclear Effects Project Officer for the Ballistic Missile Defense Office of the Advanced Research Projects Agency. After retiring from the U. S. Army in 1967, Mr. Dolan worked as a physicist at the Illinois Institute of Technology Research Institute for one year, and then managed the Nuclear Studies Program at Stanford Research Institute (later SRI). In 1981, he joined Lockheed Missiles & Space Company. Mr. Dolan's experience includes fabrication of special nuclear components in the laboratory, as well as analytical studies. He has published over 70 technical papers and reports, including several on both nuclear weapons proliferation and assessments of the nuclear technologies of existing nuclear powers; publications include U.S. Army FM 101-31, "Nuclear Weapons Employment" (1963), NA EM-1, "Capabilities of Nuclear Weapons" (1972), and with S. Glasstone, *The Effects of Nuclear Weapons* (1977).

Mr. Dolan received his B.S. from the United States Military Academy, West Point (1945) and his M.S. in physics from the University of Virginia (1956).

Robert Ehrlich, Ph.D.
Chairman, Physics Department
George Mason University
Fairfax, VA 22030

Robert Ehrlich is currently Chairman of the Department of Physics at George Mason University, and his research specialty is elementary particle physics. He was formerly Chairman of the Department of Physics at the State University of New York at New Paltz; prior faculty appointments include those at the University of Pennsylvania and Rutgers University. Dr. Ehrlich has written fifteen articles and two books. His most recent book, *Waging Nuclear Peace*, is a text to be used in university courses dealing with nuclear war. He recently chaired the nuclear winter Panel at the Health Physics Society's short course on "The Health Physics Aspects of Nuclear Attack."

Dr. Ehrlich received his Ph.D. in Physics from Columbia University (1963).

Russell P. Gates, II
Federal Emergency Management Agency
500 C Street, SW
Washington, D.C. 20472

Mr. Gates has been in the Air Force Reserves as a Communications Officer since 1965. Since

1975, he has been a Senior Engineer at Union Carbide, and has served in this capacity at the Oak Ridge National Laboratory (1978-1984). While at Oak Ridge, Mr. Gates provided experimental instrumentation in the Advanced Instrumentation for Reflood Studies (AIRS). Reflood was an international program designed to improve reactor safety. He also worked on the flux monitoring system for the breeder reactor. Since 1982, he has been actively involved in Electromagnetic Pulse (EMP) protection for communications systems. Mr. Gates is currently EMP program manager in the State and Local Programs and Support Directorate of the Federal Emergency Management Agency Headquarters.

Mr. Gates received his B.A. (1965) and his M.P.A. (1974) from West Virginia College of Graduate Study.

Leon Gouré, Ph.D.
Science Applications, Inc.
PO Box 1303
1710 Goodridge Dr.
McLean, VA 22101

Dr. Gouré was born in Russia and lived in Germany and France before coming to the United States in 1940. He is a political scientist and a specialist in Soviet studies, particularly in the areas of U.S.S.R. defense and foreign policies. During World War II, he served in the U.S. Army Counter-Intelligence Corps. He has been a student of the Soviet Civil Defense program since the 1950s and has served as a consultant to the Federal Emergency Management Agency and its predecessor agencies, as well as the Department of Defense and the State Department. Dr. Gouré is the author of numerous books and articles, among them a number of widely recognized studies of Soviet Civil Defense, such as *War Survival Strategy: U.S.S.R. Civil Defense*, and *Shelters in Soviet War Survival Strategy*. Currently he is the Director of the Center for Soviet Studies of Science Applications, Inc.

Dr. Gouré is a graduate of Columbia University and Georgetown University.

Jack C. Greene
Route 4, Box 85 A
Bakersfield, NC 28705

Mr. Greene worked with the Manhattan District in Oak Ridge during World War II and was a member of the Atomic Energy Commission's Radiation Instrument Branch from 1947 to 1951, at which time he joined the newly-created Civil Defense Agency. Since that time, he has been associated with Civil Defense-related technical and scientific activities, including radiological instrument development, nuclear weapons test programs, and other research. From 1962 to 1973, he headed the Post-Attack Research Division, which included responsibility for Civil Defense fallout studies. In 1973, he became the DCPA's Deputy Assistant Director for Research until his retirement from Civil Service in 1974. Currently, he is a consultant to the National Council on Radiation Protection and Measurements, and works with the RADEF and post-attack programs of the Federal Emergency Management Agency.

Mr. Greene received his B.S. in Electrical Engineering from Massachusetts Institute of Technology (1947), and his Master's degree in Engineering Administration from George Washington University (1970).

Sumner A. Griffin, Ph.D.
School of Agriculture
Tennessee Technological University
Cookeville, TN 38505

Dr. Griffin began working with radioisotopes in farm animals in 1951. He worked for Mallinckrodt Chemical Works in Animal Health and Nutrition (1955-1957), and he was a member of the faculty of Animal Science at the University of Tennessee during 1957-1970. At Oak Ridge National Laboratory, from 1967 to 1970, he worked with Civil Defense research concerning vulnerability of food and agriculture to nuclear attack. Since 1970, he has served as Dean of the School of Agriculture at Tennessee Technological University.

Dr. Griffin received his B.S. from Cornell University (1949), his M.S. from the University of Kentucky (1950), and his Ph.D. from Michigan State University (1955).

Major Arthur T. Hopkins
United States Air Force

Major Hopkins has served as a Nuclear Effects Project Officer with the Defense Nuclear Agency. His current doctoral program research involves the incorporation of real winds into fallout modeling codes.

Major Hopkins received an M.S.E. in Aerospace and Atmospheric Sciences from the Catholic University of America (1973), and an M.S. in Nuclear Engineering from the Air Force Institute of Technology (1982), where he is currently completing his Ph.D. degree.

Stanley Kronenberg, Ph.D.
CSTA Laboratory
Radiac Division, DELCS-K
Fort Monmouth, NJ 07703

Since 1953, Dr. Kronenberg has been employed by the U. S. Army in Fort Monmouth, where he is currently a Senior Research Physicist. He also serves as a consultant to the Federal Emergency Management Agency in the area of Civil Defense radiological instrumentation. He is a highly trained specialist in nuclear radiation physics and has worked extensively in the areas of nuclear instrumentation, dosimetry, and nuclear radiation effects. He has participated as a Project Officer in numerous nuclear weapons tests. He has published 46 scientific papers and holds nine patents. He is a member of the American Physical Society. Dr. Kronenberg has received 15 science awards, including the Meritorious Civilian Service Medal (Department of the Army, 1960), and the Army Research and Development Achievement Award in 1961, 1972, and 1976.

Dr. Kronenberg received his Ph.D. in Physics from the University of Vienna in Austria (1952).

Edward Lessard
Brookhaven National Laboratory
Upton, NY 11973

Edward Lessard is a Health Physicist with the Brookhaven National Laboratory, which he joined in 1977 as Training Supervisor for the Safety and Environmental Protection Division. From 1980 to the present, he has been Program Manager for the Marshall Islands Radiological Safety and Internal Dosimetry programs. He and his staff evaluate the radiological impact of United States nuclear weapons testing on people in the Pacific Ocean areas. Mr. Lessard is a member of the Health Physics Society, the American Nuclear Society, and he is the President of the Greater New York Chapter of the Health Physics Society.

Mr. Lessard received both B.S. and M.S. degrees in Radiological Sciences and Protection from the University of Lowell (Massachusetts).

Howard D. Maccabee, M.D., Ph.D.
2900 Hurlston Court
Walnut Creek, CA 94598

Dr. Maccabee is currently the Medical Director of the Radiation Oncology Center in Walnut Creek, CA. He has extensive experience in the field of radiation physics, and has served as a consultant to numerous organizations involved in the areas of radiation physics, medicine, and bio-medical aspects of nuclear energy. He has published numerous articles pertaining to the health effects of radiation. He is President of Doctors for Disaster Preparedness (U.S.A.); his article in *Emergency Management Review*, "Medical-Ethical Argument for Civil Defense," provided a strong argument for preparedness in response to the highly publicized television special, "The Day After."

Dr. Maccabee received his Ph.D. in Nuclear Engineering/Medical Physics from the University of California-Berkeley, and his M.D. from the University of Miami School of Medicine.

Stan Martin
Stan Martin & Associates
860 Vista Drive
Redwood City, CA 94062

Mr. Martin has enjoyed a long professional career in one of the modern inter-disciplinary arenas of applied research, namely fire research-- the study of destructive fires and explosions, and research in the development of means to prevent or mitigate their effects on man and his environment. His career, which started in the early 1950s at the Naval Radiological Defense Laboratory in San Francisco and which spans more than thirty-five years of continuous focused study, began with the measurements of thermal radiation from the fireballs of atmospheric nuclear explosions, and was followed by impressively diverse experimental and analytical efforts to understand and forecast the incendiary potential of nuclear weapons. Subsequently, at URS Research Company and then Stanford Research Institute, Mr. Martin's activities branched into peace-time concerns for fire and explosion safety. In 1982, he left his position of Director of SRI's Fire Research Department to found his own company, which provides consulting and research services in the field of fires and explosions.

Mr. Martin is a graduate of San Jose State College (CA), where he began his formal training as a chemist.

Fred A. Mettler, Jr., M.D.
Albuquerque Veterans Administration Medical Center
2100 Ridgecrest Dr. SE
Albuquerque, NM 87108

Dr. Mettler is Vice-Chairman of the Department of Radiology at the University of New Mexico School of Medicine, and Chief of Radiological Services at the Albuquerque Veterans Administration. He is a Diplomate of the National Board of Medical Examiners and is licensed in New

York, New Jersey, Illinois, Montana, California, Kansas, Pennsylvania, and New Mexico. He received certification from both the American Board of Radiology and the American Board of Nuclear Medicine. Dr. Mettler is a member of numerous medical and scientific societies, and committees, including his active membership in the National Council on Radiation Protection and Measurements Scientific Committee #63, Radiation Exposure Control in a Nuclear Emergency. He has over 100 publications, including medical journal contributions, books and monographs.

Dr. Mettler received his A. B. in Mathematics from Columbia University (1966), his M.D. from Jefferson Medical College (1970), and his M.P.H. from Harvard School of Public Health (1975).

Jiri Nehnevajsa, Ph.D.
University Center for Social Research
University of Pittsburgh
Pittsburgh, PA 15213

Dr. Nehnevajsa has been a Professor of Sociology at the University of Pittsburgh since 1961, where he was Chairman of the Department from 1962 to 1966 and 1970 to 1971. He was a Visiting Professor at the Universities of Heidelberg (1967-1968) and Mannheim (1968), as well as at the Chinese University of Hong Kong (1970-1971) and the Chinese Academy of Social Sciences (1979, 1980, 1981). He was a Visiting Scientist at the National Science Foundation, Policy Research and Analysis Division during 1980-1981. For over twenty years, he has conducted research on credibility and acceptance of Civil Defense measures; on peace and war issues; and on natural and technological hazards, including seven nation-wide surveys. He serves as an associate member of the Civil Defense Committee of the FEMA Advisory Board (since 1982), is a frequent lecturer in the National Emergency Management Training Institute programs, and he has chaired the "acceptance" group in the Project Harbor Civil Defense study. During 1966-1969, he was a member of the Civil Defense Committee of the National Academy of Sciences. He has also carried out numerous international studies of socio-political and economic changes. His most recent publication (with B. Holzner) is *Organizing for Social Research*.

Hillyer Norment, Ph.D.
Atmospheric Science Associates
PO Box 307
363 Great Road
Bedford, MA 01730

Dr. Norment has developed models for the Nuclear Defense Agency which represent the state-of-the-art in close-in fallout prediction from nuclear explosions. Models at three levels of sophistication are represented: (a) DELFIC is a detailed numerical model for research use which can also serve as a comparison standard for simpler models; (b) SIMFIC is a much-simplified numerical model that is designed to give adequation prediction accuracy for most purposes, whereas, compared with DELFIC, its data input and computer requirements are slight; and (c) DNAF-1 requires evaluation of simple analytical equations. It is designed to provide very rapid predictions from minimum data input so that it can be used for large-scale damage assessment and war-gaming studies. Currently, Dr. Norment is writing a chapter on Residual Radiation for the Defense Nuclear Agency *Nuclear Effects Manual*.

Warren K. Sinclair, Ph.D.
National Council on Radiation Protection
  and Measurements
7910 Woodmont Ave., Suite 1016
Bethesda, MD 20814

Dr. Sinclair is President of the National Council on Radiation Protection and Measurements, a private, non-profit organization which was chartered by the United States Congress and which publishes reports on all aspects of radiation protection. Dr. Sinclair was Senior Biophysicist at the Argonne National Laboratory, and also served there as Associate Laboratory Director for Biomedical and Medical Research. He had a distinguished teaching career at the University of Chicago and the University of Texas. He is past President of the Radiation Research Society and of the American Association of Physicists in Medicine. He has published more than 125 original scientific papers, and personal research has included a variety of studies in medical physics, in biophysics and radiobiology, in cellular aspects of radiation effects, and in radiation protection and risk estimation. He has been or is active in a long list of professional organizations and activities; the importance of his extensive professional contributions are given tribute by the many honors bestowed upon him.

Dr. Sinclair received a B.Sc. degree and a M.Sc. degree with Honors in Physics in New Zealand. He received his Ph.D. in Physics from the University of London.

George Sisson
4004 Ingersol Drive
Silver Spring, MD 20902

Mr. Sisson was Project Engineer for a brief time for the gas division of a public utility; subsequently he was employed by the U. S. Air Force as a civil engineer specializing in foundations for the Nuclear Weapons Effects Test Program. He served as Chief of the Soils Branch in the Air Force Special Weapons Center Structures Division, and later, as Chief Scientific Advisor for that Division. In 1963 he joined the Office of Civil Defense as a structures engineer, and he was Director of the Shelter Research Division in the Research Directorate of the Office of Civil Defense from 1967 to 1979. He is now retired.

Following army service in the southwest Pacific area in World War II, Mr. Sisson received a B.S. in Civil Engineering from Ohio State University (1949).

Paul Skierkowski, Ph.D.
Radiation Safety Office
905 Asp, Room 108
Norman, OK 73019

Dr. Skierkowski's military service (1963-1967) included special training as a nuclear weapons officer. From 1971 to 1982, he was Professor of Pharmaceutics and Radiation Safety Officer at the University of Mississippi. Since 1982, he has been Radiation Safety Officer and Adjunct Professor at the University of Oklahoma.

Dr. Skierkowski received a B.S. in Pharmacy (1963), an M.S. (1969), and a Ph.D. in Bionucleonics (1971) at Purdue University.

Kenneth Skrable, Ph.D.
Graduate School
Radiation Laboratory
University of Lowell
Lowell, Massachusetts 01854

Dr. Skrable is currently Professor of Radiological Sciences at the University of Lowell. He has applied health physics experience in a variety of settings, and has performed research, training, and consulting for a number of private and public concerns.

Dr. Skrable received his B.S. in Physics from Moravian College (1958); he was an AEC Health Physics Fellow in 1958-1959. He received his M.S. from Vanderbilt University (1964), and his Ph.D. from Rutgers University (1969).

Richard Small, Ph.D.
Pacific-Sierra Research Corporation
1456 Cloverfield Blvd.
Santa Monica, CA 90404

Dr. Small has held faculty positions at the Technion-Israel Institute of Technology (1971-1978), Tel Aviv University (1975-1977), and the University of California-Berkeley (1977-1979). Since 1979, he has been Senior Engineer at Pacific-Sierra Research Corporation. He has performed experimental and theoretical research in applied optics, separated flows, viscous supersonic flows, potential flows, heat transfer, transonic aerodynamics, and fire physics. He has published over 40 technical papers and reports, and has been invited to present lectures at several seminars and conferences. His biographical sketch is included in *Who's Who in the West, Who's Who in Science and Technology*, and *Who's Who in Aviation and Aerospace*.

Dr. Small received his Ph.D. from Rutgers University (1971).

Lewis V. Spencer, Ph.D.
PO Box 87
Hopkinsville, KY 42240-0087

After completing his graduate research, Dr. Spencer began work at the National Bureau of Standards on problems of gamma ray penetration. His study of energy loss and angular distributions led to the development of a method utilizing spatial and angular moments and polynomials, which provided high accuracy solutions to problems without boundaries. There resulted afterward a series of papers and monographs that presented high quality penetration data, applicable to many types of shielding problems. Subsequently he published a series of papers which developed early high-quality data for electrons, followed by publications on the theory of cavity ionization and related mathematical methods. Later work focused on barrier shielding against fallout gamma rays, and, in collaboration with C.M. Eisenhauer and N. FitzSimons, methods of evaluating protection factors (PF's) for structures (more generally 'identified methods which have been applied to identify and evaluate fallout shelters in government programs). In 1982, he published (with Eisenhauer and A.B. Chilton) *Structure Shielding Against Fallout Gamma Rays from Nuclear Weapons*. He has been a member and/or chaired a number of committees, and is currently Chairman of Scientific Committee #63, Radiation Exposures in Large Emergencies, of the National Council on Radiation Protection and Measurements (NCRP). He also serves on the NCRP Council, is a member of its committee on radiation transport theory, is a consultant to the radiation theory groups of NBS, and is a member of an NAS-NRC committee designated to reevaluate radiation exposure at Hiroshima and Nagasaki. He retired from Civil Service in 1984. Awards for Dr. Spencer include the U.S. Office of Civil and Defense Mobilization Distinguished Service Award (1960), the L.H. Gray Medal of the International Commission on Radiation Units and Measurements (1969), and the U.S. Department of Commerce Gold Meritorious Service Award (1972).

Dr. Spencer received his Ph.D. from Northwestern University (1948).

Daniel J. Strom, Ph.D.
Department of Radiation Health
Graduate School of Public Health
University of Pittsburgh
Pittsburgh, PA 15261

Dr. Strom is currently Assistant Professor of Health Physics, Department of Radiation Health, University of Pittsburgh. He was introduced to health physics at the Oak Ridge Associated Universities' Special Training Division for ten weeks in 1974. He was Radiation Safety Officer at the University of Connecticut Health center from 1973 to 1976, and also at the Eastern Virginia Medical School and Old Dominion University in Norfolk, VA, from 1978-1980.

Dr. Strom received his B.A. (1971) and his M.S. (1973) in Physics from the University of Connecticut at Storrs. Certified by the American Board of Health Physics in 1980, he was awarded a DOE Health Physics Fellowship for 1982-1983. His doctoral research in dose assessment work in support of the U.S. Department of Energy Health and Mortality Studies culminated in his Ph.D. degree at the University of North Carolina at Chapel Hill (1984).

Walmer Strope
Center for Planning and Research, Inc.
5600 Columbia Pike
Bailey's Cross Roads, VA 22041

Trained as a naval architect, "Jerry" Strope helped plan the first nuclear weapons test at Bikini in 1946. He became Associate Director of the U.S. Naval Radiological Defense Laboratory in 1960, and the Assistant Director for Research in the Office of Civil Defense in 1961. He retired from Civil Service in 1973, and is currently the Chairman of the Board of the Center for Planning and Research, Inc.

Lauriston S. Taylor, Sc.D.
National Council On Radiation Protection
  and Measurements
7910 Woodmont Ave., Suite 1016
Bethesda, MD 20814

Dr. Taylor has been a leader in the field of radiation protection for more than one-half century, beginning with his appointment as Chairman of the National Committee on Radiation Protection in 1929, and continuing with his position as President of the (renamed) National Council on Radiation and Protection Measurements. He retired in 1977. He is currently Honorary President of the NCRP. Dr. Taylor has held numerous prestigious positions, including Secretary of the ICRP, Secretary and Chairman of the ICRU, Chief of the AEC's Biophysics Branch, Chief of the Atomic and Radiation Physics Division, and Associate Director of the of the National Bureau of Standards. He was a Special Assistant to the President of the NAS, and Executive Director of the Academy's Advisory Committee on Emergency Planning. Dr. Taylor is also a past President of the Health Physics Society. He has received numerous awards and honors during a career in which he has written and lectured extensively on the general subject of radiation protection. He participated in several formal programs relating to the United States Civil Defense program. For several years, he was Chairman of the NAS Scientific Advisory Committee on Civil Defense, and he served as Associate Director of Project Harbor. On a number of occasions, he has been called to testify during Congressional hearings on various civil Defense subjects.

Dr. Taylor obtained his undergraduate degree from Cornell University, and later did graduate work at both Cornell University and Columbia University. He was awarded honorary Doctorates by the University of Pennsylvania and St. Procopius College.

Edward Teller, Ph.D.
Hoover Institution
Stanford, CA 94305
  or
Lawrence Livermore National Laboratory
Livermore, CA 94550

In the early 1930s, Dr. Teller taught and conducted research at Goettingen with Werner Heisenberg and at Copenhagen with Niels Bohr. During the rise of the Nazi Party, he left Germany and went to the University of London, and later to the United States, where he became a citizen in 1941. Dr. Teller has served the United States in many capacities, which include: member of the

General Advisory Committee of the U. S. Atomic Energy Commission; Chairman of the first Nuclear Reactor Safeguards Committee; member of the United States Air Force Scientific Advisory Board; member of the President's Foreign Intelligence Advisory Board; and member of the Defense Intelligence School. In 1982, he became a member of the White House Science Council. He has received many distinguished honors and awards, including the Enrico Fermi Medal, the Albert Einstein Award, the Joseph Priestly Award, the Harvey Prize, and the National Medal of Science. Dr. Teller is perhaps best known for his work on the development of nuclear explosives and for his advocacy of a strong defense for America.

Dr. Teller received his university education in Germany and was awarded his Ph.D. from the University of Leipzig (1930).

C. John Umbarger, Ph.D.
Los Alamos National Laboratory
MS 493 LANL
Los Alamos, NM 87545

Dr. Umbarger has been at the Los Alamos National Laboratory since 1971; currently, he is head of IT-1 (Instrument Technologies) at that Laboratory. He has written more than 40 publications, and has acquired two Los Alamos patents, as well as five current patent applications involving nuclear instrumentation. He has been an active participant in the annual meetings of The Tri-Service Radiac Working Group (Army, Navy and Air Force; FEMA also participates). A recent meeting (October, 1983) was held at Los Alamos; Dr. Umbarger presided as General Chairman. His research interests include low and medium energy nuclear physics, activation analysis, nuclear instrumentation development, environmental monitoring, and health physics.

Dr. Umbarger received a B.S. in Physics from Michigan Tech University (1964), and a Ph.D. in Nuclear Physics from Florida State University (1969).

Thomas E. Waterman
IITRI
10 West 35th St.
Chicago, IL 60616

Mr. Waterman is Engineering Advisor for fire and explosion research at the Illinois Institute of Technology (IIT) Research Institute and also teaches at IIT. His expertise spans most aspects of fire research. He has studied the fire hazards of building structures, interior finishes, and contents, and he has developed standard test methods for carpeting, radioactive material packaging, and mobile home finishes. His recommendations on smoke detector placement, the result of full-scale tests, have been incorporated in the National Fire Codes. His study of criteria for room flashover is recognized as a cornerstone of modern analytical and experimental studies of room fire development. As IITRI's lead person in Civil Defense fire research, Mr. Waterman has conducted programs to evaluate ignitions caused by weapons, urban area fire development, formation and fire potential of fire brands, blast/fire interactions, shelter habitability, and standardized shelf fire tests. Many of these studies have involved instrumented fire experiments in actual structures.

Mr. Waterman received his B.S. (1952) and his M.S. (1954) degrees from the Illinois Institute of Technology.

Hubert Wilson
Oak Ridge National Laboratory
PO Box X
Oak Ridge, TN 37830

Mr. Wilson for many years served as Development Engineer in the Instrumentation and Controls Division at the Oak Ridge National Laboratory. He has worked in the Radiation Detection Group, with concentrated efforts in health physics and Civil Defense-type instrumentation. During the past two years, he has devoted his time to the Civil Defense instrumentation program.

Mr. Wilson received a B.S. in Mechanical Engineering and a B.S. in Electrical Engineering from the University of Tennessee.

GLOSSARY

[This Glossary is adopted from *The Effects of Nuclear War*, whose glossary was excerpted from the larger one in *The Effects of Nuclear Weapons*, 3rd ed., Samuel Glasstone and Philip J. Dolan, Eds., prepared and published by the U.S. Department of Defense and the U.S. Department of Energy, Washington, D.C., 1977.]

Alpha Particle: A particle emitted spontaneously from the nuclei of some radioactive elements. It is identical with a helium nucleus, having a mass of four units and an electric charge of two positive units.

Cloud Column: The visible column of weapon debris (and possibly dust and water droplets) extending upward from the point of burst of a nuclear (or atomic) weapon.

Crater: The pit, depression, or cavity formed in the surface of the Earth by a surface or underground explosion. Crater formation can occur by vaporization of the surface material, by the scouring effect of air blast, by throwout of disturbed material, or by subsidence. In general, the major mechanism changes from one to the next with increasing depth of burst. The apparent crater is the depression which is seen after the burst; it is smaller than the true crater (i.e., the cavity actually formed by the explosion), because it is covered with a layer of loose earth, rock, etc.

Dynamic Pressure: The air pressure that results from the mass air flow (or wind) behind the shock front of a blast wave. It is equal to the product of half the density of the air through which the blast wave passes and the square of the particle (or wind) velocity behind the shock front as it impinges on the object or structure.

Electromagnetic Pulse (EMP): A sharp pulse of radio frequency (long wavelength) electromagnetic radiation produced when an explosion occurs in an unsymmetrical environment, especially at or near the Earth's surface or at high altitudes. The intense electric and magnetic fields can damage unprotected electrical and electronic equipment over a large area.

Fallout: The process or phenomenon of the descent to the Earth's surface of particles contaminated with radioactive material from the radioactive cloud. The term is also applied in a collective sense to the contaminated particulate matter itself. The early (or local) fallout is defined, somewhat arbitrarily, as those particles which reach the Earth within 24 hours after a nuclear explosion. The delayed (or worldwide) fallout consists of the smaller particles that ascend into the upper troposphere and into the stratosphere and are carried by winds to all parts of the Earth. The delayed fallout is brought to Earth, mainly by rain and snow, over extended periods ranging from months to years.

Firestorm: Stationary mass fire, generally in built-up urban areas, causing strong, in-rushing winds from all sides; the winds keep the fires from spreading while adding fresh oxygen to increase their intensity.

Fission Products: A general term for the complex mixture of substances produced as a result of nuclear fission. A distinction should be made between these and the direct fission products or fission fragments that are formed by the actual splitting of the heavy-element nuclei. Something like 80 different fission fragments result from roughly 40 different modes of fission of a given nuclear species (e.g., ^{235}U or ^{239}Pu). The fission fragments, being radioactive, immediately begin to decay, forming additional (progeny) products, with the result that the complex mixture of fission products so formed contains over 300 different isotopes of 36 elements.

Gamma Rays (or Radiations): Electromagnetic radiations of high photon energy originating in atomic nuclei and accompanying many nuclear reactions (e.g., fission, radioactivity, and neutron capture). Physically, gamma rays are identical with x rays of high energy, the only essential difference being that x rays do not originate from atomic nuclei but are produced in other ways (e.g., by slowing down [fast] electrons of high energy).

Height of Burst (HOB): The height above the Earth's surface at which a bomb is detonated in the air. The optimum height of burst for a particular target (or area) is that at which it is estimated a weapon of a specified energy yield will produce a certain desired effect over the maximum possible area.

Kiloton Energy: Defined strictly as 10^{12} calories (or 4.2×10^{12} joules). This is approximately the amount of energy that would be released by the explosion of 1,000 kt (1 million tons) of TNT.

Neutron: A neutral particle (i.e., with no electrical charge) of approximately unit mass, present in all atomic nuclei, except those of ordinary (light) hydrogen. Neutrons are required to initiate the fission process, and large numbers of neutrons are produced by both fission and fusion reactions in nuclear (or atomic) explosions.

Nuclear Radiation: Particulate and electromagnetic radiation emitted from atomic nuclei in various nuclear processes. The important nuclear radiations, from the weapons standpoint, are alpha and beta particles, gamma rays, and neutrons. All nuclear radiations are ionizing radiations, but the reverse is not true. X rays, for example, are included among ionizing radiations, but they are not nuclear radiations since they do not originate from the nucleus.

Nuclear Weapon (or Bomb): A general name given to any weapon in which an explosion results from the energy released by reactions involving atomic nuclei, either fission or fusion or both. Thus, the A-(or atomic) bomb and the H-(or hydrogen) bomb are both nuclear weapons. It would be equally true to call them atomic weapons, since it is the energy of atomic nuclei that is involved in each case. However, it has become more or less customary, although it is not strictly accurate, to refer to weapons in which all the energy results from fission as A-bombs or atomic bombs. In order to make a distinction, those weapons in which part, at least, of the energy results from thermonuclear (fusion) reactions of the isotopes of hydrogen have been called H-bombs or hydrogen bombs.

Overpressure: The transient pressure, usually expressed in pounds per square inch, exceeding the ambient pressure, manifested in the shock (or blast) wave from an explosion. The variation of the overpressure with time depends on the energy yield of the explosion, the distance from the point of burst, and the medium in which the weapon is detonated. The peak overpressure is the maximum value of the overpressure at a given location and is generally experienced at the instant the shock (or blast) wave reaches that location.

Rad: A unit of absorbed dose of radiation; it represents the absorption of 100 ergs of nuclear (or ionizing) radiation per gram of absorbing material, such as body tissue. The international (SI) unit for absorbed dose is the gray (symbol Gy), where 1 Gy = 100 rad.

Rem: A unit of biological dose of radiation; the name is derived from the initial letters of the term "roentgen equivalent man (or mammal)." The number of rems of radiation is equal to the number of rads absorbed multiplied by the relative biological effectiveness of the given radiation (for a specified effect). The rem is also the unit of dose equivalent which is equal to the product of the number of rads absorbed and the "quality factor" of the radiation. The international (SI) unit for absorbed dose is the sievert (symbol Sv), where 1 Sv = 100 rem. [The rem is limited to radiation protection applications at low doses (up to 25 rem). It should not be used in assessing the effects of high- level, accidental exposures.]

Roentgen: A unit of exposure to gamma (or x) radiation. It is defined precisely as the quantity of gamma (or x) rays that will produce electrons (in ion pairs) with a total charge of 2.58×10^{-4} coulomb in 1 kilogram of dry air. An exposure of 1 roentgen (symbol R) results in the deposition of about 94 ergs of energy in 1 gram of soft body tissue. Hence, an exposure of 1 roentgen is approximately equivalent to an absorbed dose of 1 rad (0.01 Gy) in soft tissue. See Rad.

SI Prefixes: The International System (SI) of units employs prefixes with units to denote multiples of 10. These are given below:

Factor	Prefix	Symbol
10^{18}	exa	E
10^{15}	peta	P
10^{12}	tera	T
10^{9}	giga	G
10^{6}	mega	M
10^{3}	kilo	k
10^{-3}	milli	m
10^{-6}	micro	μ
10^{-9}	nano	n
10^{-12}	pico	p
10^{-15}	femto	f
10^{-18}	atto	a

Thus, for example, 1 kt = 1 kiloton = 10^3 tons = 1000 tons; 1 μCi = 1 microcurie = 10^{-6} curie = 0.000,001 curie.

Thermal Radiation: Electromagnetic radiation emitted (in two pulses from an air burst) from the fireball as a consequence of its very high temperature; essentially, it consists of ultraviolet, visible and infrared radiations. In the early stages (first pulse of an air burst), when the temperature of the fireball is extremely high, the ultraviolet radiation predominates; in the second pulse, the temperatures are lower and most of the thermal radiation lies in the visible and infrared regions of the spectrum. For high-altitude bursts (above 100,000 feet [~30,500 meters]), the thermal radiation is emitted as a single pulse, which is of short duration below about 270,000 feet (~82,000 meters) but increases at greater burst heights.

REFERENCES

[Editor's Note: For general references, the reader is directed to FEMA, 1983 and 1987; Glasstone and Dolan, 1977; NCRP, 1974; NCRP, 1982; NAS, 1975; and OTA, 1979]

Barber, G.R., Sisson, G.N. *Crisis Blast Shelter Planning Guide*. Center for Planning and Research, September, 1982.

Bauer, E. "Dispersion of Tracers in the Atmosphere and Ocean: Survey and Comparison of Experimental Data." *Journal of Geophysical Research* 79:789, 1974.

Bell, M.C., Blake, A.C. "Fallout Facts for Milk Producers." University of Tennessee Agricultural Extension Service RCD - 14 January 1976.

BEIR III Report: see National Academy of Sciences, 1980.

Bigelow, W.S. "Far Field Fallout Prediction Techniques." Ph.D. dissertation, Air Force Institute of Technology, Dec. 1983. Available from University Microfilms, Ann Arbor, Michigan.

Billheimer, J.W., Jones, F.J., and Meyers, M. "Food Support of the Relocation Strategy." Prepared for the Defense Civil Preparedness Agency by SYSTAN, Inc., Los Altos, CA, September 1975.

Billheimer, J.W., et al. "Post-attack Impacts of the Crisis Relocation Strategy on Transportation Systems." Prepared for the Defense Civil Preparedness Agency by SYSTAN, Inc., Los Altos, CA, September 1978.

Billheimer, J.W. and McNally, J. "Guidelines and Data to Support Plans for Reallocating Food During Crisis Relocation." Prepared for the Federal Emergency Management Agency by SYSTAN, Inc., Los Altos, CA, December 1982.

Billheimer, J.W. and McNally, J. "Transportation Planning Guidelines for the Evacuation of Large Populations." Prepared for the Federal Emergency Management Agency by SYSTAN, Inc., December 1983.

Bridgman, C.J., Bigelow, W.S. "A New Fallout Prediction Model." *Health Physics* 43:205-218, 1982.

Broido, A., McMasters, A.W. "The Influence of a Fire-Induced Convection Column on Radiological Fallout Patterns." California Forest and Range Experiment Station, Berkeley, CA, March, 1959.

Caldwell, M.M. *Bio. Sci.* 29:520, 1979.

Chang, J.S., Duewer, W.H., Wuebbles, D.J. *Journal of Geophysical Research* 84:1755, 1979.

Cronkite, E.P., Bond, V.P., Dunham, C.L. "A Report on the Marshallese and Americans Accidentally Exposed to Radiation from Fallout and a Discussion of Radiation Injury in the Human Being." In: *Some Effects of Ionizing Radiation on Human Beings*. U.S. Atomic Energy Commission, USAEC-TID 5358. Washington, D.C.: U.S. Government Printing Office, 1956.

Defense Nuclear Agency. "Fact Sheet: Nuclear Test Personnel Review." Washington, D.C.: DNA Public Affairs Office, April 3, 1984.

Defense Nuclear Agency, et al. *Proceedings of the Conference on Large Scale Fire Phenomenology September 13-18, 1984, Gaithersburg, MD*. Defense Nuclear Agency, Federal Emergency Management Agency, and Center for Fire Research of the National Bureau of Standards. In press, 1985.

Eisele, G.R., Bell, M.C. "Bacterial and Hematological Evaluation of Cattle Exposed to Lethal Gamma Radiation." *Radiat. Res.* 53:462-467, 1973.

Eisele, G.R., Griffin, S.A. "Problems of Livestock Salvage." In: *Annual Progress Report, Civil Defense Research Project, March 1968-March 1969*. USAEC Report ORNL-4413, Part 1, pp. 97-100, Oak Ridge National Laboratory, October 1969.

Eisele, G.R., Griffin, S.A. "Problems of Livestock Salvage." In: *Civil Defense Research Project Annual Progress Report, March 1969-March 1970*. USAEC Report ORNL-4566, Part 1, Oak Ridge National Laboratory, 1970.

Eisenbud, M. *Environmental Radioactivity*, 2nd ed., New York: Academic Press, 1973.

Federal Emergency Management Agency (FEMA). Civil Preparedness Guide CPG 1-6, *Disaster Operations Handbook for Local Governments*.

FEMA -- Federal Emergency Management Agency. *Radiation Safety in Shelters*. Washington, D.C.: U.S. Government Printing Office, 1983.

FEMA -- Federal Emergency Management Agency. *Attack Environment Manual.* 9 volumes, 1987.

Fruchter, J.S. et al. "Mount St. Helens' Ash from the 18 May 1980 Eruption: Chemical, Physical, Mineralogical, and Biological Properties." *Science* 209:1116-1125, 1980.

Glasstone, S. and Dolan, P.J. *The Effects of Nuclear Weapons.* 3rd edition. No. 008-046-00093-0. Washington, D.C.: U.S. Government Printing Office, 1977.

Gogolin, J.H. "Method for Calculating the Fractional Rate of Radioactivity Deposition for a Range of Yields and Various Particle Size Activity Distributions." M.S. Thesis, Air Force Institute of Technology, Dayton, Ohio, 1984. D.T.I.C. No. AD 141066.

Griffin, S.A. "Vulnerability of Livestock and the Livestock Industry." *Annual Progress Report, Civil Defense Research Project, March 1967 - March 1968.* ORNL - 4282, Part I, 1968.

Griffin, S.A. "Vulnerability of Livestock to Fallout Radiation," *Annual Progress Report, Civil Defense Research Project, March 1968 - March 1969.* ORNL-44-13, Part I, 1969a.

Griffin, S.A. "Livestock Vulnerability to Fallout Radiation." *American Society of Agricultural Engineers.* ORNL-69-842, 1969b.

Griffin, S.A., Bressee, J.C., A.F. Shinn. "The Vulnerability of Food to Nuclear Attack." In: *Proceedings of the Symposium on Radiological Protection of the Public to Nuclear Mass Disaster, Interlaken, Switzerland, May 26-June 1, 1968.* International Radiation Protection Association, pp. 589-607, 1969.

Griffin, S.A., Eisele, G.R. "Problems in Post-attack Livestock Salvage: Survival of Food Crops and Livestock in the Event of Nuclear War." In: *Proceedings of a Symposium, Brookhaven National Laboratory.* pp. 269-276, 1971.

Hopkins, A.T., Bridgman, C.J. *Journal of Geophysical Research* 90:10620-10630, 1985.

ICRP -- International Commission on Radiological Protection. *Recommendations of the International Commission on Radiological Protection.* ICRP Report 26. Oxford: Pergamon Press, 1977.

James, R.A. *Estimate of Radiation Dose to Thyroids of Rongelap Children Following the BRAVO Event.* Lawrence Radiation Laboratory Report, Livermore, C.A., UCRL-12273, 1964.

Kearny, C.H. *Trans-Pacific Fallout and Protective Countermeasures.* Oak Ridge National Laboratory (ORNL-4900), November 1973.

Kossakowski, S. "The Investigations on the Possibility of Vital Diagnosis of Post-Radiation Autoinfection in Slaughter Animals." *Vet. Med. (Poland)* 24:449-453, 1968 (In Polish). *Nuclear Science Abstracts* 224:877, January 15, 1970.

Lane, W.B., Lee, H. "Effects of Mass Fires on Fallout Deposition." SRI Project MV-6824, OCD Work Unit 3124B, NRDL-REC-68-22, February 1968.

Lessard, E.T., Miltenberger, R.P., Cohn, S.H., Musolino, S.V., Conrad, R.A. "Protracted Exposure to Fallout: the Rongelap and Utirik Experience" *Health Physics* 46:511-527, 1984.

Lessard, E.T., Miltenberger, R.P., Conrad, R.A., Musolino, S.V., Naidu, J.R., Moorthy, A., Schopfer, C. *Thyroid Absorbed Dose for People at Rongelap, Utirik and Sifo on March 1, 1954.* BNL 51882. Brookhaven National Laboratory, Upton, N.Y., 1985.

Lushbaugh, C.C. "The Development and Present State of the DOE Health and Mortality Studies." In: *Program and Working Papers: DOE Radiation Epidemiology Contractors Workshop, April 13-14, 1982.* Robert Goldsmith, Ed. USDOE Human Health and Assessments Division, Office of Health and Environmental Research, Office of Energy Research, 1982.

Luther, F.M. *Nuclear War: Short Term Chemical and Radiative Effects of Stratospheric Injections.* Lawrence Livermore National Laboratory Report UCRL-89957, 1983.

MacCracken, M.C., Chang, J.S. "A Preliminary Study of the Potential Chemical and Climatic Effects of Atmospheric Nuclear Explosions." Lawrence Livermore National Laboratory Report UCRL-51653, 1975.

Mettler Jr., F.A., Moseley Jr., R.D. *Medical Effects of Ionizing Radiation.* Orlando, FL: Grune & Stratton, Inc., 1985.

Murphy, H.L. et al. *Feasibility Study for Slanting for Combined Nuclear Weapons Effects.* (3 volumes). Stanford Research Institute, October, 1975.

NAS -- National Academy of Sciences. *Long-Term Worldwide Effects of Multiple Nuclear Weapons Detonations.* Washington, D.C.: National Academy Press, 1975.

NAS -- National Academy of Sciences. *The Effects on Populations of Exposure to Low Levels of Ionizing Radiation: 1980 Committee on the Biological Effects of Ionizing Radiations (BEIR).* ("BEIR III Report"). Washington, D.C.: National Academy Press, 1980.

NCRP -- National Council on Radiation Protection and Measurements. *Radiological Factors Affecting Decision-Making in a Nuclear Attack.* NCRP Report No. 42. Washington, D.C.: NCRP, 1974.

NCRP -- National Council on Radiation Protection and Measurements. *The Control of Exposure of the Public to Ionizing Radiation in the Event of Accident of Attack.* Proceedings of an NCRP Symposium on April 27-29, 1981. Bethesda, MD: NCRP, 1982.

Neir, A.O.C. *Long-Term Worldwide Effects of Multiple Nuclear-Weapons Detonations.* A report by a committee of the National Academy of Sciences/National Research Council. Washington, DC: National Academy Press, 1975.

OTA -- Office of Technology Assessment. *The Effects of Nuclear War.* Washington, D.C.: U.S. Government Printing Office, 1979.

Parrish, B.A. *Evaluation of External Personnel Monitoring Devices and Data for Oak Ridge National Laboratory Epidemiological Study.* Masters' technical report, Department of Environmental Sciences and Engineering, School of Public Health, University of North Carolina at Chapel Hill, 1982.

Pawel, O., Kalousova, V., Vranovska, J. "Results Obtained in Microbiological Tests of Meat and Slaughtered Swine Afflicted by Radiation Sickness." *Vet. Med. (Prague)* 12:361-366, 1967.

Rumpf, H. *Brandbomben.* Berlin: E.S. Mittler u. Sohn, 1931.

Rumpf, H. *Der Hochrote Hahn.* Darmstadt (FRG): E.S. Mittler u. Sohn, 1952.

Schell, J. *The Fate of the Earth.* New York: Knopf, 1982.

Schull, W.J., Otake, M., Neel, J.V. "Genetic Effects of the Atomic Bomb: A Reappraisal." *Science* 231:1220-1227, 1981.

Shleien, B. *Preparedness and Response in Radiation Accidents.* U.S. Department of Health and Human Services, HHS Publication FDA 83-8211. Washington, D.C.: U.S. Government Printing Office, 1983.

Silverman, M.S., Bond, V.P., Greenman, V., Chin, P.H. "Bacteriological Studies on Mice Exposed to Supralethal Doses of Ionizing Radiations. I. Radiation from a Nuclear Device." *Radiat. Res.* 7:270-276, 1957.

Sisson, G.N. "Mining More Protection." *Foresight,* May-June, 1975.

Spencer, L.W., Chilton, A.B., Eisenhauer, C.M. *Structure Shielding Against Fallout Gamma Rays From Nuclear Detonations.* National Bureau of Standards Special Publication 570. National Bureau of Standards, Department of Commerce, Washington, D.C., September 1980.

Strom, D.J. *A Strategy for Assessing Radiation Monitoring Data from Many Facilities for Use in Epidemiologic Studies.* Doctoral dissertation, Department of Environmental Sciences and Engineering, School of Public Health, University of North Carolina at Chapel Hill, 1984. Available from University Microfilms, Ann Arbor, Michigan.

Strong, A.B., Smith, J.M., and Johnson, R.H. "EPA Assessment of Fallout in the United States from Atmospheric Nuclear Testing on September 26 and November 17, 1976, by the People's Republic of China." United States Environmental Protection Agency, Office of Radiation Programs, (EPA-520/5-77-002), August 1977.

Takata, A.N., Waterman, T.E. *Fire Laboratory Tests--Phase II: Interaction of Fire and Simulated Blast Debris.* OCD Work Unit 1135A, Contract DAHC 20-70-C-0406. IITRI Project J6217, February, 1972.

Texas A & M. *Rural Shelter Handbook.* Texas A & M University, Texas Agricultural Extension Service, College Station, Texas, undated.

TTAPS -- See Turco, et al.

Turco, R.P., Toon, O.B., Ackerman, T.P., Pollack, J.B., Sagan, C. "Nuclear Winter: Global Consequences of Multiple Nuclear Explosions." *Science* 222:1283-1292, 1983. Known as *TTAPS*.

UNSCEAR, The United Nations Scientific Committee on the Effects of Atomic Radiation. *Sources and Effects of Ionizing Radiation: UNSCEAR 1977 Report.* Report to the General

Assembly, with annexes, United Nations, New York, New York, 1977. Available from UNIPUB, 10033-F King Highway, Lenham, MD 20706.

UNSCEAR, The United Nations Scientific Committee on the Effects of Atomic Radiation. *Ionizing Radiation: Sources and Biological Effects -- UNSCEAR 1982 Report.* Report to the General Assembly, with annexes, United Nations, New York, New York, 1982. Available from UNIPUB, 10033-F King Highway, Lenham, MD 20706.

Wasserman, R.H., Trum, B.F. "Effect of Feeding Dogs the Flesh of Lethally Irradiated Cows and Sheep." *Science* 121:894-896, 1955.

Waterman, T.E. *Fire Laboratory Tests--Phase I.* OCD Work Unit 1135A, DAHC 20-70-C-0406, IITRI Project J6183, September, 1970.

Waterman, T.E. *Fire Laboratory Tests--Phase III: Fire in Blast Initiated Debris External to Shelters.* OCD Work Unit 1135A, Contract DAHC 20-70-C-0406, IITRI Project J6217, February, 1973.

Waterman, T.E. *Fire Laboratory Tests--Effects of Barrier Integrity and Fire Ventilation on Shelter Habitability.* OCD Work Unit 1135A, DAHC 20-70-C-0406, May, 1974.

particle size	xi, 5, 11, 47, 74
Penalty Table	53
PF (protection factor)	x, 14, 15, 29, 30, 33, 56, 67
plutonium (see also ^{238}Pu, ^{239}Pu, etc)	4, 5, 7-9, 12, 17-21, 61
potassium iodide (KI)	2, 13, 50, 51
protection	iii, x, xi, xii, xiii, 1-3, 6, 10, 13-16, 23-26, 29, 30, 31, 33, 38, 41, 43, 48-50, 52, 53, 56, 57, 59, 61, 62, 64-68, 72, 74, 75
protection factor (PF)	x, 29, 30, 38, 56
public	vii, xi, 1, 3, 5-7, 21, 23, 25, 31, 43-46, 49, 51, 53, 60, 61, 66-68, 73-75
radiation risk (see also risk)	55
radiochromic waveguide	35, 36
reactor	ix, 4, 12-14, 18-20, 50, 61, 62, 64, 69
relocation	ix, 13, 24-26, 43, 44, 46, 58, 73
risk	2, 5, 6, 14, 23-26, 30, 31, 39, 41, 44, 46-50, 53, 54, 55-57, 66
Rongelap	4, 6, 7, 37-39, 74
"salted weapons"	x, 32, 33
seven-ten rule	28
shelter	2, 8, 13, 14, 25, 26, 30, 33, 38, 39, 46, 48, 49, 52, 56-62, 67, 69, 73, 75, 76
slanting	49, 50, 74
SNM	18-20
strontium (see ^{90}Sr)	13
surface burst	10, 11
thyroid	xii, 2, 37, 38, 50, 51, 74
transport	1, 2, 9, 19, 62, 68
transuranics (see also TRU)	5-7
^{238}Pu	5, 19
^{239}Pu	4, 5, 8, 18, 19, 71
^{241}Am	4, 5
TRU	5-7
TTAPS	21, 22, 45-47, 75
U.S.S.R.	7, 8, 25, 26, 31, 64
underground	48, 61, 71
uranium	
^{233}U	18, 19
^{235}U	4, 18, 71
^{238}U	4, 18
Utirik	37-39, 74
ventilation	48, 49, 56, 60, 76
warning times	x, xi, 31
weapons-grade plutonium	4, 7, 8, 20
wind	2, 11-13, 27-29, 32, 38, 40, 71
wrist-watch	xiii, 35-37, 59, 60
x radiation	5, 34, 49
x ray	11, 71, 72

INDEX

^{131}I	2, 37, 50
^{132}I	50
^{137}Cs	7, 39
^{232}Th	18, 19
^{233}U	18, 19
^{235}U	4, 18, 71
^{238}Pu	5, 19
^{238}U	4, 18
^{239}Pu	4, 5, 8, 18, 19, 71
^{240}Pu	4, 5, 19
^{241}Am	4, 5
^{241}Pu	4, 19
^{242}Pu	19
^{60}Co	7, 15, 32, 39
^{90}Sr	7, 9, 39
air burst	6, 10, 12, 72
alpha	ix, 4-9, 61, 71, 72
americium (see ^{241}Am)	4
animals	xi, 5, 33, 34, 55, 64, 74
ANWT (atmospheric nuclear weapons test)	4, 7, 8
army instruments	34-37
atomic bomb (see also nuclear weapon)	x, 43, 75
attack	iii, v, viii, ix, x, xi, xii, 1-9, 11-16, 22-34, 38, 40, 41, 44, 46-53, 55-58, 61, 63, 64, 73-75
background	iii, 19, 20, 35, 36, 39, 53, 54, 59, 60
beta	4, 9, 18, 33, 37, 59, 72
Bikini	4-6, 39, 68
biological effects	ix, x, 53, 75, 76
blast	9, 12-15, 17, 21, 23-25, 38, 41, 43, 44, 47-52, 56, 57, 59, 69, 71-73, 75, 76
cancer	xii, 5, 6, 30, 38-40, 43, 47, 48, 53, 55, 58
caves	xii, 48
CdTe (cadmium telluride)	36, 59
Civil Defense	iii, vii, viii, x, xi, xii, 1-3, 14, 22-27, 29, 31, 34, 35, 43-47, 49, 56-62, 64-69, 73, 74
cobalt bomb	xi, 32
cockroaches	16
deposition	xi, 1, 2, 5, 7-11, 27, 32, 40, 41, 72, 74
detectors	14, 15, 36, 53, 59, 60
DOE	1, 54, 55, 62, 68, 74
dosimeter	34-37
Dr. Strangelove	32
EMP (electromagnetic pulse)	x, 23, 64, 71
Enewetak	4-7, 39, 61
EPA	1, 2, 6-8, 75
evacuation	2, 3, 25, 31, 32, 46, 50, 56-58, 73
Mississauga	3
fallout	ix, x, xi, xii, 1, 2, 4-15, 17, 24, 25, 27-41, 43, 44, 46-50, 52, 56-58, 62, 64, 66, 67, 71, 73-75
FCDA	56, 57
FEMA	1, 35, 61, 62, 66, 69, 74
fire	xii, xiii, 3, 25, 40, 41, 50, 52, 57, 59, 60, 65, 67, 69, 71, 73, 75, 76
fireball	1, 9-11, 47, 72
fires	xi, 21, 40, 41, 52, 57, 59, 60, 65, 71, 74
firestorm	40, 41, 71
fission	ix, 2, 4, 6, 7, 9-13, 19, 27, 29, 34, 50-52, 71, 72
food	1, 3, 6, 7, 16, 23, 25, 37, 38, 46, 50, 61, 62, 64, 73, 74
fusion	27, 51, 72
gamma	5, 6, 9, 11, 14, 15, 19, 30, 32-37, 39, 42, 47, 51, 52, 59, 60, 67, 71-73, 75
genetic	xii, 16, 30, 55, 56, 75
genetic effects	xii, 55, 75
gnat	16
ground burst	21, 27
ground zero	6, 7
GZ (ground zero)	6, 7
heat	xiii, 46, 51, 52, 56, 57, 59, 67
HgI (mercury iodide)	59
Hiroshima	5, 6, 11, 16, 17, 19, 41, 57, 68
immune system	xi, 42
INR (initial nuclear radiation)	6, 16, 17, 34-36, 61
insects	iii, x, 1, 15, 16, 62
instruments	xi, 14, 30, 31, 34-36, 57, 59
iodine (see ^{131}I, ^{132}I)	
KI (potassium iodide)	2, 13, 50, 51
livestock	xi, 33, 73, 74
lymphocyte	42, 43
Marshall Islands	xi, 4, 37, 39, 65
mines	xii, 31, 48, 49
Mississauga	3
model	14, 21, 22, 28, 45, 47, 54, 57, 66, 73
Nagasaki	6, 11, 17, 20, 57, 68
NaI (sodium iodide)	14
NCRP	xii, 30, 47, 52, 53, 67, 68, 73, 75
neutron	xii, 4, 5, 9, 18-20, 32, 34, 36, 37, 51, 52, 61, 71
neutron bomb	xii, 6, 51, 52
Nevada Test Site	8, 47, 61
NO$_x$	58
nuclear attack	iii, v, ix, x, xi, xii, 1-4, 6-9, 14, 15, 22, 23, 25, 27, 28, 30-34, 40, 41, 44, 46-52, 55-58, 61, 63, 64, 74, 75
nuclear power	ix, 12, 31, 61
nuclear reactor (see reactor)	
nuclear weapon	4, 5, 7, 8, 12, 18-21, 31, 33, 40, 50, 51, 53, 61, 72
nuclear winter	x, xi, 6, 16, 21, 22, 31, 45, 46, 63, 75
OCDM	57
ozone	xii, 31, 58, 59

77